W0010363

THIS BOOK BELONGS TO

_____

52
DEVOTIONS
FOR DOG
LOVERS

BroadStreet
PUBLISHING

BroadStreet Publishing Group LLC
Savage, Minnesota, USA
Broadstreetpublishing.com

52 DEVOTIONS FOR DOG LOVERS

978-1-4245-6501-6 (faux)
978-1-4245-6502-3 (ebook)

Devotional entries composed by Michelle Cox, Carol Hatcher, Lori Brown, Jessica Chenoweth, Edie Melson, and Sylvia Schroeder.

Design and typesetting by Garborg Design Works | garborgdesign.com
Editorial services by Michelle Winger | literallyprecise.com

Printed in China.

22 23 24 25 26   5 4 3 2 1

INTRODUCTION

Dogs are called man's best friend for a reason. They're loyal. They protect us. They give us love. They're happy to see us when we return home. And who can resist those furry faces and wagging tails?

We think we own them, but truth be told, it might be more accurate to say that they own us. Many canines have us trained to do their bidding. When they show us some doggy affection, we're perfectly fine with them being in charge.

Dogs sense when we're not feeling well, and they excel at giving comfort. That's why they're so good as service or therapy dogs. Oh, the joy they bring! What could be finer than an afternoon playing with our dogs or sharing a walk on a perfect day?

Dogs also provide us with wonderful spiritual and life lessons. That's what you'll find in the pages of this book. Each chapter contains a devotion, a prayer, a Bible verse, a question for reflection, and a Did you know....

Curl up with your favorite pup and enjoy reading about the God-moments we discover while hanging out with our furry canine friends.

I WILL LOVE YOU

The Lord has appeared of old to me, saying:
"Yes, I have loved you with an everlasting love;
Therefore with lovingkindness I have drawn you."

JEREMIAH 31:3 NKJV

My friend, Lynn, had been excited all day long. A special delivery was flying in for her and she couldn't wait. She was supposed to pick the delivery up early in the afternoon, but there was a flight delay. Then there was another delay, and another, until it was after midnight that she headed to the airport.

She was tired but excited to meet the newest members of her family—two rescue dogs. Both had been mistreated and abandoned. Lynn knew they had scars, both physically and emotionally. She was nervous about the days ahead, but ever since she'd seen their photos and read their stories on the adoption center's website, she'd known they were *her* dogs. Without even meeting them, she'd fallen in love with the pair. Her heart was touched and pained by all they'd been through.

After a long travel day, the dogs were tired and nervous as well. Lynn spoke softly to them and stroked their fur with gentle hands. She whispered, "I know things have been bad in the past, but you have a forever home with me now, and I'm going to show you nothing but kindness and love. You'll see."

It took a while for the wounded dogs to trust her, but as time went by and she fed them and gave them loving attention, they began to thrive. Their once lackluster fur gleamed from her care. Their tails wagged with joy, and they played with carefree abandon. They knew they were loved.

In much the same manner, the Almighty God looked down from heaven and spotted us, wounded by circumstances and desperate for someone to love us. His heart was touched by us and pained by all we'd been through. He whispered, "I know things have been bad in the past, but I have a forever home for you, and I love you enough that I gave my life for you. You are mine."

With tender care, he brought joy into our lives. He fed us with mercy and grace. His gentle, nail-scarred hands brought healing into our once-wounded hearts. And we knew we were loved.

Dear Lord, the wounds of my past have affected me in so many ways. There have been times when I felt like I was on the fringe as I watched others who were loved and whose lives seemed so blessed. Then you stepped into my life and showed me that I could trust you. You treated me with kindness and patience, even though I messed up so many times. You healed the broken places in my heart and filled them with your love. How do I even begin to express my gratitude? Words don't suffice. Thank you for the gift of your love and the promise of a forever home with you.

PAWS TO THINK

How has the assurance of God's
love changed you?

DID YOU KNOW

*There are nearly fourteen thousand
animal shelters and rescue groups
across North America.*

TRUE BEAUTY

Do not let your adorning be external—the braiding of hair
and the putting on of gold jewelry, or the clothing you wear—
but let your adorning be the hidden person of the heart
with the imperishable beauty of a gentle and quiet spirit,
which in God's sight is very precious.

1 Peter 3:3-4 esv

Cindy has a miniature dog named Princess. Princess has a precious little face, fluffy fur, and is downright adorable. She is even cuter when Cindy dresses her in little doggy clothes—beachwear, rainwear, Christmas sweaters, and frilly outfits. Princess wears them with pride, and the cuteness quotient is off the charts!

Princess gets noticed everywhere she goes. Sometimes, it's for the cowgirl outfit she's wearing, or for the princess dress and tiny dog tiara. Friends on social media share photos of Princess, and likes on the photos sometimes number into the thousands.

Princess wasn't always so cute. She was once a rescue dog—unwanted and dirty, her fur was matted and muddy.

With the love and care of her new master, the previously unkempt dog became a stunning creature.

Though outward beauty and cute clothing are what folks notice first, after they are around Princess for a while, they discover something else that makes them love her even more. The little dog is affectionate and well-behaved. She loves everyone equally, from the janitor at the school to the millionaire at the coffee shop. Her inner beauty far outshines what is on the outside.

The same is true for us. There's nothing wrong with fixing our hair and makeup and wearing pretty outfits. The problem comes when we spend more time on that than we do working on our inner beauty.

What if we put as much effort into our hearts and souls as we did with our daily beauty routines? What if we cleansed away the imperfections that keep us from being like God? What if we clothed ourselves with kindness and love?

God thinks a gentle and quiet spirit is beautiful. As many of us have discovered, outward beauty fades, wrinkles appear, and hair thins and turns gray. Inner beauty will never perish—and it will always please the heart of our Master.

Father, the desire of my heart is to be beautiful for you. Help my character to reflect yours. Give me a depth of kindness and love for others to make me an extension of your loving hands. Remind me to work on my inner beauty routine—to spend time in your Word, to get rid of my imperfections through repentance and confession to you, and to clothe myself in your love. Give me a quiet and gentle spirit so that whenever people look at me, they'll see a reflection of you.

PAWS TO THINK

Think of three people who excel at inner beauty. What makes them inwardly beautiful? What can you do to enhance your inner beauty?

DID YOU KNOW

Dog grooming is not just for cosmetic appeal; it's important for their health.

TAKE A TASTE

O taste and see that the Lord is good;
How blessed is the man who takes refuge in Him!

Psalm 34:8 NASB

I couldn't believe what I was seeing. As a new bride, I was still honing my cooking skills. I'd tried my first batch of fried chicken that evening, and I was thrilled because everything had turned out perfectly. The chicken was golden brown and crispy. It looked like something out of a magazine. I put the platter of fried chicken on the table and turned around to finish dishing up the vegetables.

When I turned to place the vegetables on our kitchen table, I let out a scream that made my husband come running.

We had purchased a house up the street from my in-laws. It didn't have a screen door, but it was warm that afternoon, so I'd opened the door to get some air. When I turned around to place the vegetables on the table, I discovered my father-in-law's beagle, Ouncie, had trotted up the street to see us. He'd climbed on a chair and was eating my fried chicken!

He's not the only dog who sneaks a bite of food. My friend had a huge St. Bernard named Lucy. She was so big that her head could comfortably reach the counter. One night, my friend left the kitchen for a few minutes while her stir fry cooked. When she returned, she discovered Lucy had stuck her head in the wok and eaten half of the contents.

Another time, Lucy polished off a platter of brownies. On a third occasion, Lucy devoured tater tots from a take-out restaurant.

When dogs are hungry, they dive right into what is in front of them.

What if we were that hungry for God's Word? What if we devoured those pages with the same delight as hungry dogs? A feast of promises, comfort, advice, and instructions for living are right in front of us. A heaping helping of inspiration, worship, and praise are ours for the taking. And for dessert, there are sweet moments where God sits with us and whispers to our souls.

Isn't it time we followed Ouncie and Lucy's examples and helped ourselves to what God has waiting for us?

Father, I'll be honest. I know I don't read my Bible like I should. If I do, it's in hurried little snatches. It's your love letter to me, yet I allow it to gather dust. Please give me a hunger for your Word. Help it to come alive for me. Help me to see things I've never noticed before. Open up time for me to savor what I'm reading, to allow the words to seep into my soul and make a difference in my life. I don't want to miss the messages you have for me. Thank you for this precious gift.

PAWS TO THINK

Why don't you read your Bible more often? How can you gain a hunger for God's Word?

DID YOU KNOW

Chocolate, macadamia nuts, cooked onions, or anything with caffeine can be harmful to dogs. evidently that didn't bother Lucy's bulk when she gobbled up brownies and stir fry!

WAiTING FOR YOU

Let us not grow weary while doing good,
for in due season we shall reap if we do not lose heart.

GALATIANS 6:9 NKJV

Our family has a home in Florida with a guest cottage behind it. Our son and his family live in the house. My husband and I use the cottage when we are in town, and we get daily visits from our grandchildren—and also our grand-dog, Gus. He comes over every morning. My husband lets him in, and that small black ball of fur hops up on the bed with me for snuggles.

Gus is a sweet dog. He's good with the kids, doesn't disturb anything (most of the time), and he's a vocal guard dog whenever someone comes near the house. He's a member of the family, and he loves hanging out with everyone.

On one of our visits, some friends were in the cottage, so we stayed in the house. After we left, my daughter-in-law sent me a picture of Gus standing at the front door, waiting for us to come back. She said he sat there for hours. I loved that.

On our next trip, we stayed in the cottage. Gus again made regular visits to see us. And then after we returned home, my daughter-in-law sent a picture that totally melted my heart. Gus was standing patiently on the porch of the cottage, waiting for us to come back.

Did you catch that? Gus was waiting patiently. That's a lesson most of us could learn. I'll admit I've often been guilty of praying about something and then getting impatient when the answer didn't arrive as fast as I thought it should.

I've learned a valuable lesson the past few years. Just because an answer doesn't arrive on my timetable, it doesn't mean that God isn't busy on my behalf. In fact, if the answer arrived when I expected it, important pieces of God's plan wouldn't have been in place. His idea was bigger than mine, and the waiting was necessary to accomplish it.

I don't want to rush God. Instead, I want to be like little Gus, waiting patiently.

Father, my instinct is to want answers immediately when I pray about something. I'll be honest, I don't like waiting. As I wait, help me to learn the lessons you want me to learn. Remind me that you're often busily at work, even when I can't see anything happening. I want to fulfill the desires of your heart for me. Help me to be faithful in the waiting. Encourage my heart and help me not to rush you and your plans. May I encourage others who are also waiting for the answers by sharing stories of how you've always been faithful to me.

PAWS TO THINK

Why is it sometimes so hard
to wait on God?

DID YOU KNOW

The "wait" command tells your dogs to stay put and not move forward until you release them.

BEST IN SHOW

Whatever you do, do it heartily, as to the Lord and not to men, knowing that from the Lord you will receive the reward of the inheritance; for you serve the Lord Christ.

<small>COLOSSIANS 3:23-24 NKJV</small>

Excitement filled the event center on the day of the dog show. Behind the scenes was a whirlwind of activity. Owners washed and groomed their prize dogs, making sure their coats gleamed, every hair in place. Some partners had done this so many times, they knew exactly what to do. For others, it was their first time at the show. Still, nervous excitement was evident in everyone.

Months of hard work had led to this day. Intensive grooming. Good nutrition to obtain optimum health. Many hours of training to perform before the judges. Best in show doesn't happen by chance—and the competition is fierce.

Various breeds were led onto the floor, one at a time. The judges inspected them carefully, comparing them to the other dogs in the ring and to the standard for their breed. It was apparent quickly that some weren't going to make the grade, but others stood out immediately, both for their beautiful form and for a certain aura that made them shine.

The judges watched as the handlers put their dogs through their routines, trotting around the ring. Nerves were evident, and some didn't display as well as anticipated. Others did far better than expected, the countless hours of training paying off.

Then came the nail-biting moment when the winners were announced. The crowd cheered loudly as proud owners congratulated their dogs.

In our Christian lives, we can't expect to be best in show without putting in hard work. Becoming more like Christ isn't easy. We need intensive grooming to repent of and resist the sin and impurities in our lives. We need the right nutrition—countless hours in God's Word—to achieve optimal spiritual health. God must train us and mold us into his desired form.

God mentions some of his winners for us in the Bible. Job, whom he defined as a perfect and upright man. David, a man after God's own heart. Abraham, who was called a friend of God. These winners were not perfect, and they only succeeded through their Lord. That put them in God's best in show—and they are inspiring examples of what we can become in Christ.

Lord, I want to become what you desire for me—and yet I often fall short of that. I get sidetracked by life. I realize that it takes consistent effort for me to be ready to stand before you. Give me a firm commitment to study your Word. Groom me so my life is clean and gleaming for you. I want to become more like you each day. Train me and mold me. I would love to be one of your best in show—not for my glory, but so others can see you in me.

PAWS TO THINK

What specific steps can you take to become a woman after God's own heart?

DID YOU KNOW

Every year, during Westminster Week, the Empire State Building partakes in the celebration by lighting up in purple and yellow—the official colors of the Westminster Dog Show.

WHAT TO DO

Then they cried to the LORD in their trouble,
And He brought them out of their distresses.

PSALM 107:28 NASB

Like most teenage girls, we were talking and laughing as we walked through the neighborhood. Caught up in each other's company, we didn't pay much attention to our surroundings—until I looked down the street and gasped. I'm sure my face was white as I pointed to show my friends.

Most of the neighborhood yards had fences, but one didn't. A huge German shepherd had run out to the street from that house and he was headed our way. And judging by the menacing growls, the frenzied barking, and the sharp teeth poised to tear into us, it wasn't for a quick pet.

We all stopped in our tracks—mainly because we were too afraid to move. The dog stopped as well. One of my friends whispered, "I don't know what to do."

That's when someone said, "Pray!" Trust me when I say I was already doing that!

Over the loud barking, we heard a voice yell, "The dog will bite!"

We'd kind of figured that out already. When I could get my voice to work, I hollered, "Could you come and get your dog?" She walked slowly from her porch—it seemed like five weeks to us as the hound continued to snarl at us—and finally took him into the house.

Our legs were shaking too much to run, but once we got out of there, we never visited that street again. The dog was just protecting his property, but it was a frightening experience.

There have been so many days in my life when I haven't known what to do and when circumstances overwhelmed me. I couldn't see any answers to my problems. When we faced that protective dog, I learned that prayer can make a huge difference. Whenever I don't know what to do, that should be my first step not my last resort. I'm so grateful for a God who hears my frantic prayers and rescues me when I need him.

Dear Father, there are so many occasions when I don't know what to do. Thank you for always hearing my prayers and for responding to them. Help me to reach out to you first instead of worrying or complaining. You've done amazing things for me and solved problems that seemed unsolvable. Thank you for being my rescuer and protector. I love you, Lord, and I don't ever want to take that for granted. I'm so grateful for a faithful God who never leaves me defenseless.

PAWS TO THINK

What are some situations where God has rescued you? What did you learn?

DID YOU KNOW

Dogs are called man's best friend because of their boundless loyalty and willingness to protect their owners.

SMILE THERAPY

A cheerful heart is good medicine,
but a crushed spirit dries up the bones.

PROVERBS 17:22 NIV

My little granddaughter hadn't smiled in several days. Stuck in unfamiliar surroundings and emotionally scarred by a traumatic event, her normally sunny personality had disappeared. I knew how she felt. With knots in my stomach and a cloud of worry over me, I hadn't felt like smiling either.

Days earlier, I arrived in Colorado to speak at a conference. My phone rang as I sat down in the shuttle, and I was devastated to learn that my two-year-old granddaughter, Ava, had been rushed to the hospital because of a seizure. I was alone, far from home, and so worried.

When I learned she had a second seizure at the hospital, I was even more upset. My son sent a picture of Ava in her hospital gown. She looked so unwell and so tiny, and I sat there and cried as I prayed for her.

It was finally decided that the seizures had occurred

due to a high fever. The news was a relief, but my heart still ached for my baby girl as pictures continued to arrive and she looked so sad.

Then came the photo that brought back the sunlight. A therapy dog visited the hospital, and my son said the minute the pup pranced through the door, Ava started smiling. The picture showed Ava with her arms wrapped around the fluffy dog. He'd broken through her fear and brought comfort. I can't tell you how much I wanted to hug that dog!

I am grateful for a God who has so often broken through my sadness and fear. A God who is with me when my world falls apart. A God who is always present when I can't be with my loved ones.

I'm thankful for the gift of prayer and the difference it makes to go to Jesus when I don't know what to do. I'm grateful for the provision of a sweet therapy dog who brought comfort and a smile to my beloved granddaughter.

Lord, I don't know how I'd survive life if I couldn't come to you in prayer. Thank you for hugs from heaven whenever my world falls apart. Thank you for listening when I pour my heart out to you. I'm grateful that when I can't be with those I love, I have the sweet assurance that you will be with them no matter where they are. Thank you for always providing what is needed—even when part of the answer to my prayers comes in the form of a fluffy therapy dog.

PAWS TO THINK

Why is a cheerful heart
like good medicine?

DID YOU KNOW

Therapy dogs are dogs that bring comfort and joy to people in poor conditions, such as those affected by a natural disaster or an illness. Many people are able to connect with dogs and feel the love that they provide, and this boosts their mental and physical wellbeing.

BE MY FRIEND?

A friend loves at all times,
And a brother is born for adversity.

PROVERBS 17:17 NASB

Hisses and howls often erupt when cats and dogs are in the same room. At our house, it was mostly from the cat, because the poor dog was just trying to be friendly. Let's just say his overtures of friendship didn't go over too well and he exited the room with a few scratches on his nose. But things were different at Jennie's house. Her dog and cat were buddies.

Their close friendship became evident one day when Jennie couldn't find her cat. Jennie looked everywhere, calling for the kitty as she went from room to room. The search went on for hours. Jennie was worried that she'd run away somehow.

Jennie's cat-obsessed dog had been pacing from her bedroom to the living room for hours too, but she thought it was because the dog was feeling her anxiety. Every time

Jennie would sit down, the dog would place her paw on Jennie's lap and then go pace again.

Jennie finally said, "Where is your kitty?" The dog stood up, went into the bedroom, and pointed like a hunting dog at the dresser. Jennie followed her and opened the dresser drawer, and the cat popped out. It seems Jenny had accidentally closed the dresser drawer on her, not realizing that the cat had snuggled down in there.

But her dog knew the whole time, and he didn't give up on helping his friend until that kitty was rescued.

All of us need a friend like that—and Jesus is our most reliable friend. He never leaves us. He knows where we are at all times, and he rescues us when we're in trouble. He loves us and wants to be with us. He hears our whispered prayers and his heart is touched by what concerns us.

Friend, if you don't have a personal relationship with Jesus, you're missing out on the best friendship ever. When Jesus enters your heart, you gain a friend who will be with you every moment of your life.

Lord, I'm so grateful that you're my friend. It humbles me that you want to be friends with me. I never have to worry about you leaving me. I never have to worry that you won't be there when I need to pour out my problems and receive wise counsel. Thank you for always rescuing me. Father, I want to be a good friend to you as well. Help me to be faithful and to listen when you speak to my heart. I want to follow your example and be a good friend to others who need one.

PAWS TO THiNK

How can you be more like Jesus in your friendships with others?

DiD YOU KNOW

The most successful mountain rescue dog in history was a St Bernard named Barry who lived during the early 1800s and saved forty lives.

FAITH OF A CHILD

"With God nothing will be impossible."

LUKE 1:37 NKJV

We often talk to our children about faith, but the best way for them to learn about faith is to see it in action. Sometimes we're afraid to put God to the test. Maybe we're afraid he won't answer. Perhaps we're so busy trying to fix things ourselves that we simply don't think to ask him for help. A little girl named Lindsey can teach us a valuable lesson about faith.

Susan's daughter, Lindsey, was eight. The family had adopted a dog from the pound, and Lindsey adored that little pup. All was well until the first of January when the dog disappeared from their fenced yard. Lindsey was devastated. They posted signs, searched, and offered a reward, but Muffin was still missing.

February arrived, and the dog hadn't returned home. On February 2nd, the night before her birthday, Lindsay asked, "Mama, can God do anything?"

Her mother replied, "Yes, baby, he can."

"Well, I prayed and asked God to bring Muffin home for my birthday."

Susan tucked her in and then got down on her knees for some fervent prayer. She knew this was a milestone of faith for her daughter. But they woke on Lindsey's birthday to no Muffin. Lindsey was so disappointed.

Susan went out to warm the car before they left for school. When she looked up, a ten-pound fur ball was running toward her as hard as she could. By the time the dog reached the steps, all of them were in tears. To this day, Lindsey will tell you that God brought back Muffin for her birthday.

Friends, sometimes we need the faith of a child. We know God can do anything, so why don't we bring our requests to him? Sometimes his answer isn't immediate. Sometimes it's a no, and sometimes God amazes us.

Do you have an impossible need today? Maybe it's time to take it to the God who always has answers.

Lord, I often try to fix my problems myself. I stress. I worry. I never bring those problems to you until I've done all I know to do. And yet nothing is impossible for you. Remind me to place my circumstances into your capable hands. Give me the faith of a child and help me to trust you even when I don't see the answer. Give me patience until your time is right and help me to share my stories of a faithful God who excels at the impossible.

PAWS TO THINK

What do you think Lindsey learned from God answering her prayer of faith? What can you discover from that?

DID YOU KNOW

The average dog can run about nineteen miles per hour at full speed.

TRAIN UP A PUPPY

As newborn babes, desire the pure milk of the word,
that you may grow thereby.

1 Peter 2:2 nkjv

A friend's dog had a litter of puppies. My three sons were in heaven as they played with the wriggling little creatures. Our oldest son laughed as a tiny tongue swiped across his cheek. Our youngest son played chase with another, laughing as the furry little guy caught him. Our middle son sat quietly, holding a sleeping puppy in his lap.

Instead of getting a full-grown, housebroken dog, we came home with a puppy. Not the quiet puppy that slept on my son's lap, but one of the rambunctious ones. I should have known!

Roscoe was adorable. My heart had melted when I saw his joyful face. But at 3:00 a.m., Roscoe wasn't quite as cute to this tired mama. Once the house had quieted, the puppy decided he didn't like being alone. The whimpers went on for hours.

I started housebreaking him the next day, and I cleaned

up multiple accidents. Roscoe spilled his water. Three times. Plus, that little rascal tore the newspaper into hundreds of pieces before I discovered his handiwork. It was like having another child to care for.

Then I found that Roscoe's sharp teeth had gnawed on my favorite shoes. My husband thought it was funny until he discovered that his down pillow had fallen prey to those little teeth as well. Roscoe couldn't deny the feathers caught in his fur.

Yes, we'd brought a puppy home—one that had to mature and be trained. Fast forward a few years with me to a different story. Roscoe was housebroken. He didn't bother anything. His obedience training had paid off. Instead of all work, he was all pleasure.

It's the same way with us as Christians. When we're newly converted, we're still spiritual babies. We have to spend time in God's Word and in prayer so that we'll mature. We need to become part of an active church, listening to sermons and music that will feed our souls. We need people who will mentor and disciple us, so we can grow and thrive.

Once we've matured in our faith, we have a responsibility to bring people in, nurturing and investing in them as others invested in us. Let's not remain baby Christians but grow to be a pleasure to God and others.

Father, I'm so often like that puppy. I do wrong and mess up, even when I don't mean to. I'll never forget the joy of the day you came into my life as my Lord and Savior. I so wanted to please you, but I didn't know how. You left a guide for me in your Word and brought people into my life who cared enough to mentor me. You sent sermons that helped me grow, fellowship that strengthened my heart, and music that made me worship you. I don't want to stay a baby Christian. Help me to grow spiritually, so I become the woman you want me to be.

PAWS TO THINK

What steps can you take to help you mature in Christ?

DID YOU KNOW

Dogs are mentioned fourteen times in the Bible.

BE STILL

"Be still, and know that I am God."

PSALM 46:10 NIV

Labradors and dishwashers don't mix. April found out the hard way. Her black Lab, Abbey, watched carefully as she loaded the dishwasher, just in case she dropped a crumb or two. April finished loading and left it open when she walked into the dining room to check for more plates.

When she returned to the kitchen, she caught Abbey pre-washing a few plates as she licked them clean. Knowing she wasn't supposed to lick the plates, Abbey backed away as soon as she realized April was returning—only the dishwasher rack was caught on Abbey's collar.

As the Lab backed up, the rack full of dirty dishes yanked out of the dishwasher. Everywhere she moved the rack moved with her. Scared to death, Abbey began shaking her head and jumping around the kitchen. The rack hung on, but the dirty dishes went flying as she shook. As dishes crashed and broke around her, April tried catching her dog to unhook her. But Abbey was too scared and took off running—rack and all.

April's husband came to the rescue. He was able to catch Abbey in the living room and separated the rack from her collar. But dirty, broken plates were scattered everywhere. What a mess!

Sometimes, we are like Abbey. When fear overtakes us, we jump and shake and run. We make a huge mess instead of letting the loving hands of our Father untangle us. When we are still and recognize the sovereignty of God, our problems pale in comparison to his strength.

Often we think we are running from the problem when we are really running from the solution—God. When we feel caught in a messy situation, we need to stop and ask our Father for help. He will come to our rescue if we stop and stand still before him.

Dear Lord, sometimes I let fear get the best of me and I end up making a mess. Help me remember that you are an all-knowing and all-powerful God. Show me how to be still before you. It is so difficult to do in our hectic world. Please give me your peace that passes understanding and allow me to be calm in the face of adversity. If I've gotten myself in a mess because I was licking plates I wasn't supposed to lick, open my eyes to see the error of my ways.

PAWS TO THINK

What are some ways you can practice being still before the Lord?

DID YOU KNOW

The phrase "raining cats and dogs" came from the 17th century in England, when it rained so hard that stray cats and dogs came floating down the street.

FURRY BLESSINGS

"I have come that they may have life, and have it to the full."

JOHN 10:10 NIV

I didn't realize how much my children wanted a dog until my son asked my husband to marry another wife. My husband and children were pet lovers, but me—not so much. Puppies definitely pulled at my heart strings, but the thought of one living in my home had my blood pressure on the rise.

My son Colin told my husband to marry a woman who loved dogs. "Two wives are fine," he reasoned. "Jacob in the Bible married Rachel and Leah. And God knew all about it."

I stood firm. No dogs. After my friend's son, who had epilepsy, got a seizure response dog, my son wished to have epilepsy. I knew we had a problem, and unfortunately, the problem was me. I kept telling my family that we'd get one someday. But someday never came, until a close friend died.

When my friend died, I faced the reality that God never promises us tomorrow. So, I held my breath and jumped into dog ownership with both feet. We adopted a three-year-old yellow Labrador named Comet.

One Sunday afternoon, we returned from church to let Comet out of her crate to play. The kids ran around the yard and threw a ball for her to chase. Giggles floated through the air, and I captured the moment with a photo. Then I noticed that we were all still wearing our church clothes. We had forgotten the urge to change because we were so excited about playing with Comet.

God meant it when he said we were to live life fully. He doesn't want us to live our lives in fear. Instead, he wants us to have lives full to overflowing. Sometimes, our blessings come when we aren't afraid to say yes.

God knew better than I did—not only what I needed, but what I wanted. I didn't realize what fun I had been missing by not having a four-legged family member. God is a good father who knows how to give good gifts to his children. Sometimes, a good gift comes with four legs and a wagging tail!

Heavenly Father, thank you for the good gifts you give your children. You know better than I what my heart desires. So many things in life try to take away my joy, but you, God, give it in abundance. Thank you for the life you have given me. Open my eyes to the wonderful blessings all around me. Forgive me when I don't recognize the gifts right in front of me and help me to be open to new things. Oh, and thank you for my four-legged friends!

PAWS TO THiNK

Are you missing a blessing because you are afraid to say yes?

DiD YOU KNOW

A recent scientific study shows that dog ownership leads to a longer life.

MUD PUPPY

If we are living in the light, as God is in the light,
then we have fellowship with each other,
and the blood of Jesus, his Son, cleanses us from all sin.

1 JOHN 1:7 NLT

I heard the familiar scratch at the back door and walked across the kitchen to let in our golden Labrador retriever. Thankfully, I cracked the blinds and took a peek before actually twisting the knob and allowing her inside, and I gasped in dismay.

Imagine a swirly cone of ice cream dipped in chocolate, covering every inch and dripping down the sides. Now pretend the ice cream is actually a dog and the chocolate is mud. It looked like our dog had been dipped in mud and plopped on our doorstep!

I stared, shocked. She looked at me as if to say, "You won't believe what fun I had in the back yard!" I looked out the window to find the source of the mud. As I looked across the yard, the dog ran to the corner as if to show me. There sat a wheelbarrow full of mud. It rained enough the day before to make the Georgia clay in the wheelbarrow a cool, wet sludge.

As I was trying to figure out the clean-up process, the doorbell rang. Like a beacon of light, my dog-loving best friend, Allison, just so happened to be in the area and decided to drop by. She followed me to the backyard and couldn't stop laughing. "Get the hose," she told me. "You spray, and I'll hold her still." As I sprayed the dog with the hose, mud ran off her beautiful yellow coat in streams.

Have you ever felt coated with sin the way my dog was coated in mud? Have you ever worried that you are too dirty for God? Perhaps you feel you are not welcome in the house of God because of that sin.

Don't be afraid—God is faithful and he will forgive your sins. Everyone is welcome to come to him. He is there when we need him. We come just as we are, and he cleanses us from our sin and washes us white as snow.

Lord, sometimes I'm so ashamed, and I'm afraid to come to you because I don't think you want someone as dirty as me. But in your Word, it says that Christ died for us "while we were still sinners." Thank you for loving a sinner like me. God, please wash me and make me clean. Let my heart and life be pleasing to you. Help me to remember that all of us sin, but you are faithful and forgive us of all that we've done wrong. All I need to do is ask.

PAWS TO THINK

What things could you do to stay out of the mud on a daily basis?

DID YOU KNOW

Labradors are built for water. They have a double coat to repel water, a thick, otter-like tail, and webbed feet.

FACE TiME

"Behold, I stand at the door and knock;
if anyone hears My voice and opens the door,
I will come in to him and will dine with him, and he with Me."

REVELATION 3:20 NASB

Ridge is an apricot standard poodle. While cartoons often depict them as small dogs, a full-grown poodle can grow up to 60–70 pounds. Ridge is quite a large dog. An old adage says, "Age is only a state of mind." But for dogs, it should be, "size is a state of mind," because Ridge is pretty sure he is a lap dog!

If you sit down near Ridge, he'll inch closer and closer until he's in your lap. Not only does he love to lap sit, but Ridge is also jealous of screen time. His people include a mom and dad, Laurrie and Tom, and two busy teenaged girls, Gracie and Bailey. At any given time, someone is likely to be on their electronic device—much to Ridge's chagrin.

One evening after dinner, Tom sat at the end of the table catching up on email on his phone. On the opposite end of the table, Gracie was on her laptop studying for an upcoming test. Ridge walked from Tom to Gracie and back again. Back and forth he walked, watching and waiting for one of his people to notice him. Finally, Ridge climbed up on the bench and stepped up on the middle of the kitchen table. Then he proceeded to stretch out and lay down right between Gracie and Tom.

They laughed when they looked up and noticed their furry friend, and they left their screens to give Ridge the love he needed. If dogs can sense how distracted we become, how much more does our heavenly Father notice?

We so often become preoccupied with our technology and the fast pace of life. While God doesn't climb up on our kitchen table, he does try to get our attention. He raises the sun every morning and paints the sky as it sets at night. He blows a soft breeze on our cheeks and whispers his love.

Just like our furry friends, God wants to spend more time with us—he wants to spend forever! So, let's put down our devices and pick up our Bibles today. Let's spend some time showing love to the one who created us.

Father, forgive me for being so easily distracted. I get caught up in my day-to-day life and stop noticing all the ways you love me. Thank you for sunrises and sunsets. Thank you for the beauty you created. Help me to remember to put down my phone, turn off the TV, and spend time with you. I am so grateful that you stand at the door and knock. You are always patiently waiting. God, you are worthy of all my time and all my praise.

PAWS TO THINK

How can you be more aware of the amount of time you spend on your electronic devices?

DID YOU KNOW

Dogs actually have a concept of time and miss you when you are gone.

POWER OF TOUCH

She said, "If only I may touch His clothes, I shall be made well."

MARK 5:28 NKJV

Do you ever feel like your dog has an internal DGPS (Doggie Global Positioning System)? That's what Christina thought about her dog, Curry. He had a true gift for finding his way to the beach—and he did it dragging his petite owner behind him.

Curry was Christina's foster dog. He was a boxer and loved to go on walks. Every day Christina took Curry for a two-mile walk. They lived quite close to the beach. As Christina approached the end of her block, the puppy's DGPS would kick in, and he was determined to get to the beach.

Christina is a small woman, so Curry could easily pull her along wherever he wanted to go. There was something about the sand that he loved. When they arrived at the beach, Curry would sink his paws into the sand, walk around a bit, and then allow Christina to lead him on the rest of their walk.

He never pulled her all the way to the water. It was the sand that he loved. He wanted to feel it on his paws, and he wasn't going to let little things like a leash or a lady stop him. I wonder if that's how the bleeding woman from the Bible story in Mark chapter five felt.

After twelve years of bleeding, she was desperate. This woman pushed through the crowds, thinking she could be healed if she touched the hem of Jesus' garment. She thought right, because when she did catch the edge of Jesus' robe, she stopped bleeding immediately.

Has your dog ever been determined to get to something and pulled you until he touched it? Have you ever been that desperate to get to Jesus? Whatever need you may have, a touch from the Lord can meet it. He can heal marriages, finances, fractured families, and our broken bodies—all with one touch. Reach out to him today.

When I'm faced with a problem, God, I often try to fix it on my own. If I can't fix it, I ask friends, poll social media, and do internet research. Only in desperation do I reach out to you. Oh Lord, please forgive me. You should be the first place I go when I need help. One touch from you can heal any hurt. You are almighty and all powerful. Thank you for allowing me to come to you for healing. Thank you in advance for the healing you are going to do in my life.

PAWS TO THINK

What area in your life do you
wish Jesus would touch?

DID YOU KNOW

Dogs have an incredible sense of direction. Using the earth's magnetic poles in combination with their sense of smell, they can find their way almost anywhere.

WHEN YOU NEED ME

Ruth replied, "Don't urge me to leave you or to turn back from you.
Where you go I will go, and where you stay I will stay. Your people
will be my people and your God my God."

RUTH 1:16 NIV

Our dog was surrendered by a family who was never at home. The mother was a flight attendant and decided it would be better if the dog had a place to live where she would get a little more attention. The dog was named Comet, but I've always said she should have been named Ruth.

It may sound like a strange name for a dog, but she reminded me of Ruth in the Bible. "Where you go I will go. Where you stay I will stay." Ruth refused to leave her mother-in-law, Naomi, even though she was headed to a foreign land. Ruth said she would accompany Naomi wherever she went.

I believe Comet made a similar decision. She attached herself to me immediately. I thought she was going to be an outside dog, but Comet had other ideas. I let her inside, but insisted she stay downstairs. So, every time I would go upstairs, I'd tell Comet, "Stay!" At first, she sat at the bottom of the stairs and waited for my return. But once she gained confidence, she began creeping up the stairs. Imagine my surprise when I looked down the hall to see her head laying on the top stair! Knowing she wasn't supposed to be upstairs, her body remained stretched out on the stairs below. But her chin rested on the top step as if to say, "I'm right here if you need me." Comet showed true loyalty.

We find that loyalty in Ruth for Naomi, but we really see it in God through his loyalty to the Israelites throughout the Old Testament. He has that same devotion toward us today. God promises to never leave us or forsake us.

Like our four-legged friends, God walks right beside us. He is there when we call on him and patiently waits when we become distracted. God is loyal to us, even though we don't always show the same. Let's praise God for his unwavering faithfulness and thank him for the steadfastness of our furry family members.

God, thank you for your unwavering faithfulness. You are always there for me and promise to never leave me. Forgive me, Lord, when I walk away from you. I don't deserve your love and kindness, but I am so thankful for it. Help me to be a loyal friend to the people you have put in my life. Show me ways I can demonstrate loyalty in my job. Thank you for the dependable and constant four-legged friends you have given me. Their love and devotion is a gift.

PAWS TO THINK

What are some practical ways
you can show devotion
to your family and friends?

DID YOU KNOW

Dogs are loyal because they are pack animals.
They are social and prefer the company of others.

FOUND

You are a chosen race, a royal priesthood, a holy nation, a people for his own possession, that you may proclaim the excellencies of him who called you out of darkness into his marvelous light.

1 PETER 2:9 ESV

Kate was in her first year of teaching when she decided it was the perfect time to find a dog. She was an adult now, after all. She planned to go to the pound on the weekend in hopes of falling in love. But the Friday before she was supposed to go, that plan changed drastically.

Kate was driving when noticed a puppy on the shoulder. As she drove past, the puppy stared right at her. She continued to drive, but something told her to stop her car and go back. When she got to the dog and opened her door, he ran and jumped in as if he belonged.

She drove straight to the pound and reported that she found him. Sometimes, dogs are microchipped and can be scanned for information about the owner. There's a two-week waiting period for an owner after someone turns in a dog.

The next two weeks were agonizing for Kate. She wanted the puppy to have a home, but she desperately wanted that home to be hers. The thought of someone claiming the dog was almost too much to handle. When two weeks passed, she was overjoyed to find the dog still there.

Kate quickly adopted the dog and gave him a home and a name—Finn. God does the same for us. When we accept his free gift of grace, he provides us a home in heaven and a name as a child of the King.

Have you ever felt like the abandoned puppy on the side of the road? Perhaps you've been waiting for someone to claim you and give you a home. God is driving by. Like Kate opening her door for Finn, God is waiting at an open door for you. Take some tips from Finn and run inside. You are not forgotten. You are part of a royal priesthood. You are chosen. You are found.

God, I often feel like that puppy on the side of the road. People and events in my life abandon me, but you always find me. Thank you for offering me the free gift of grace and a home with you in heaven. Thank you for allowing your Son to die for me and my sins. Forgive me when I live my life like that abandoned dog. Remind me to live like the child of the King that I am. You are an amazing Father! Praise for you will forever be on my lips. Remind me that I have been chosen. I once was lost, but now I am found.

PAWS TO THINK

Have you accepted the free gift of grace God offers? What has that meant to you?

DID YOU KNOW

No two dog noses are the same.

WHO AM I?

In Christ Jesus you are all sons of God, through faith.

Galatians 3:26 esv

Daniel and Whitney wanted a German shepherd and discussed getting one. When an old friend called and explained he had a German shepherd puppy he wanted to give them, they didn't even have to think about it. They jumped at the opportunity.

Daniel's friend explained how his other dogs weren't accepting the newest puppy, so he needed to find the dog a new home. Daniel and Whitney were thrilled; their three girls would lavish the dog with love. They took the dog in and named her Gabby. Gabby was sweet and clever and was soon house-trained.

They took Gabby to the vet for shots. They mentioned their newest family member was a German shepherd puppy. When the vet laughed, they paid no attention. They were too excited about their wonderful dog.

As the weeks passed, Whitney noticed Gabby wasn't

growing very much. German shepherds are fairly large dogs. She called the friend who gifted them the dog. The friend confirmed he had seen both of the dog's parents, and both were indeed German shepherds.

Thinking something might be wrong, Whitney headed back to the vet and shared her concerns about Gabby's small size. The doctor turned his expert eye on the pup and agreed with Whitney. Gabby was a small dog, but that was because Gabby was not a German shepherd!

Have you ever been mislabeled by the world? Everywhere you turn, someone is placing you in a category where you know you don't belong. Don't believe those lies. You are who God says you are. God says you are worthy. He loves you beyond words. That is the truth.

When others put you in a category that doesn't fit, let the expert eye of your heavenly Father look you over and proclaim truth. You are a daughter of God. You are not who the world says you are. You are who *God* says you are. Live in that truth!

Dear Lord, open my eyes to your truth. Please help me to shut out the lies the world says about me. Sometimes, I don't know what to believe about myself. It's so easy to let the lies consume me. Show me who you want me to be, and mold me into that person. Help me to see myself the way you see me, and let others see you in me. Thank you for who I am in you.

PAWS TO THINK

What lies have you been believing
about yourself?

DID YOU KNOW

Known for its intelligence, speed, agility, and stealth, the German shepherd is the preferred breed for both military and police academies.

SUPER POWER

"You shall receive power when the Holy Spirit has come upon you; and you shall be witnesses to Me in Jerusalem, and in all Judea and Samaria, and to the end of the earth."

ACTS 1:8 NKJV

Judy didn't plan on taking her grandson's dog for an ambulance ride. She also didn't plan on having a stroke. Yet the two of them set off with EMTs on an unexpected adventure to the hospital. Yes, Judy and the dog!

Judy's grandson, Spencer, had epilepsy, so he had a seizure response service dog named Lucia. When Spencer's family traveled to Florida, they left Lucia home with Grandma Judy. When Judy's daughter came to visit, she called an ambulance because Judy showed signs of a stroke. Knowing how special Lucia was, the grandma refused to leave the dog. "She's coming with us," she told the EMTs. Eyebrows raised, they agreed and off to the hospital they went.

When Judy was placed in a room, Lucia did as she was trained and found a spot to lie down. But a few minutes later, Lucia paced back and forth across the room to the door. Judy's daughter thought she needed to relieve herself and took her out. But when she returned, Lucia continued to pace.

Realizing Lucia was alerting for a seizure, Judy's daughter went in the hall to ask if someone close by had epilepsy. "Our dog is alerting that someone is going to have a seizure," she shared. Soon after, a patient in the hall began to seize.

As amazing as Lucia's abilities may be, the Holy Spirit is more powerful than predicting seizures. The power of the Holy Spirit raised Christ from the dead. The Bible tells us that gift of grace God offers includes sending the Holy Spirit to live in us. That doesn't mean you will suddenly have super powers, but it does mean you have access to the greatest power there is.

When you ask God to help you use that power to do his will, you might be amazed at what he can do. What God-sized task do you need some help with today?

Dear Lord, I struggle trying to do things with my own power. When you present me with a task, help me remember you will also equip me for that task. Please let the presence of the Holy Spirit inside me draw others to me, so I can share you with them. Let me rely on you for all things and stop trying to fix things on my own. Forgive me when I doubt your strength. Use me to do your will.

PAWS TO THINK

If there was one area in your life where you could use the power of the Holy Spirit, where would it be?

DID YOU KNOW

The first known service dogs were used by the Germans during World War I. They used German Shepherds as ambulance and messenger dogs.

PROTECTiVE POOCH

"This is how God loved the world:
He gave his one and only Son,
so that everyone who believes in him
will not perish but have eternal life."

JOHN 3:16 NLT

Dads can be overprotective when their daughters start dating. Heather's dad was no exception, but she also had a second test for her suitors. The first—did her dad intimidate you? The second—did her dog?

Not many boys could pass either test. Heather's dad was quite intimidating when it came to his daughter. Still, the hardest test to pass was the dog test. Jake was Heather's border collie, and he had a knack for sensing romance.

Some of Heather's guy friends got along just fine with Jake until they decided to move from friendship to dating. Then, Jake started all kinds of shenanigans. He frequently tried to nip the boys on the rear end, often tearing their shirts as they tried to pull away. Thankfully for the boys, Jake never broke the skin. He certainly gave a few guys a scare!

Then Kenny came along, and protective Jake never bothered him. He was able to date Heather with no nibbles or torn shirts. Kenny ended up marrying Heather, and they are living their happily ever after. It seems Jake is a great judge of character!

Aren't you grateful that we don't have to pass any tests when it comes to approaching God? He doesn't send his angels to intimidate us before we can come into his throne room. In fact, he invites us to come boldly before him.

God loved us so much that he allowed his only Son to take the test for us. Jesus lived a perfect life and died for our sins. Today's verse tells us God did this so everyone could have eternal life. All we have to do is confess those sins and believe in him. Like Heather and Kenny, we can live a happily ever after with Christ.

Heavenly Father, thank you so much for inviting everyone to come to you. When I think about your Son dying for my sins, I'm overwhelmed and grateful. Thank you. There are times I feel I can't approach you because I know that no one is worthy to do so—without Jesus. The sacrifice that Jesus made allows me that free access to you. How amazing! Help me to live my life with an attitude of thanks. Use me to do your good will.

PAWS TO THiNK

Who do you know that needs to hear the good news that Jesus died for everybody, not just a select few?

DiD YOU KNOW

Border Collies were bred to herd sheep. They are famous for using an intense stare to intimidate the flock.

TiNY ME, BiG YOU

Even there your hand shall lead me,
and your right hand shall hold me.

PSALM 139:10 ESV

Chichi was Michelle's first baby, and it was easy to see that the two of them were crazy about each other. He was the sweetest, tiniest little Chihuahua. As a young puppy, his head seemed too big for his body as if he might topple over—head first. His entire body fit in Michelle's palm.

He was a happy little puppy. When she brought him home for the first time, she took him straight outside to explore the back yard. She bent down and placed him on the grass, and the blades went past his eyeballs. Only his ears stuck up above the grass.

The grass was so tall, the tiny Chihuahua couldn't see over it. He turned this way and that with no luck. No matter which direction he turned, he was unable to see the landscape. Chichi yipped to let Michelle know he wasn't happy. Smiling at her small puppy, Michelle reached down and picked him up.

In the hands of his mother, Chichi quickly calmed down and was content. Michelle tried to place her dog back in the yard. Once again, Chichi sank into the grass jungle, and he barked until Michelle lifted him out of the grass.

Do you ever feel like Chichi? Perhaps you are overwhelmed by the circumstances around you and cry out for help. Sometimes we are put in new situations that are scary and unfamiliar. We wonder how we got there and how we will get back to normal.

Thankfully, the loving hands of our Father always guide us and hold us when we feel afraid. When we can't see where to go and every way we turn looks the same, we can call out to the one who calms every fear with a touch. God is always there to lift us when we need him.

Dear Lord, it's easy to get caught up in the trials of life and feel overwhelmed and afraid. Sometimes, I wish you would lift me out of my circumstances and place me in another section of the yard. Help me to understand that no matter where I am in the yard, there's always going to be grass around me. Thank you for coming when I call to you. Draw near to me and let me feel your presence. Show me the way you want me to go. I love you, God.

PAWS TO THINK

If you were to view your current situation
from a higher vantage point, how would
it change the way you feel?

DID YOU KNOW

*Full-grown Chihuahuas are anywhere between
two and six pounds, making them the world's
smallest breed of dogs.*

NO POUTING

Do all things without complaining and disputing.

Philippians 2:14 NKJV

It's amazing how smart dogs can be. One wouldn't think a dog would have a sense of justice or fairness. But Jax certainly did—and he let his family know he did not think they were treating him kindly.

It all started with a trip to the vet. Amanda boarded the Labrador at the vet while the family was on vacation. When Amanda returned for him a few days later, kids in tow, Jax was overjoyed to see his family again. He lavished them with doggie kisses and tail wags all the way home.

Once they walked in the house, Jax seemed to remember the same family he loved was the one who dropped him off days earlier. He lay on his bed and refused to interact with the family the rest of the evening. Whenever Amanda talked to Jax, he turned his head with a deep grumble and looked the other way. She was shocked at how much her puppy could pout.

It continued when the older boys went off to college. When they returned home for holidays or laundry runs, Jax's excitement was off the charts. He jumped and ran in circles and covered them with kisses. However, he would soon remember they left him, and the pouting would begin.

The Israelites did the same to God. They sang his praises when he delivered them from Egypt, but they soon grumbled and complained about their circumstances. Every time God delivered them, they would lose sight of his miracles in a new trouble.

It's easy to forget the blessings God has given us and focus instead on an undesirable situation. Let's not be like Jax and snub the one who loves us most. God's will is always best, and we can always find reasons to be thankful. When life is tough, we need to look for our blessings. Let's list things that are right in our lives, and soon our mouths will be filled with praises for our Father.

Dear Lord, forgive me when I am quick to forget your blessings. Too often, I pout and stomp my feet over my circumstances. Help me to remember all you have given me. You are worthy of all honor and glory and praise. When I grumble and complain, open my eyes to the many things that are good in my life. Thank you for letting me wake up today. Thank you for my home. Thank you for my family. Thank you for my four-legged friends. But most of all, thank you for loving me like you do.

PAWS TO THINK

What five blessings
can you list right now?

DID YOU KNOW

Dogs use their tails and ears to express emotion.

YOU CAN RUN

Nothing in all creation is hidden from God.
Everything is naked and exposed before his eyes,
and he is the one to whom we are accountable.

HEBREWS 4:13 NLT

My sister and I looked at each other with sudden panic as we simultaneously realized that our St. Bernard, Lucy, had escaped. This dog was a Houdini in the making and had successfully escaped from her fenced-in yard. The sun was setting, and within thirty minutes, darkness would make the search for Ms. Lucy all but impossible.

I set out on foot and my sister by car to search for Ms. Lucy. We shouted her name, drove down side streets, called neighbors, and did anything we could think of to find the 150-pound furry escapee.

After twenty minutes of searching, my phone rang. A neighbor across the street heard my sister calling Lucy's name and flagged her down to say, "I have her. She's here." Fear gave way to relief as my sister pulled into the neighbor's driveway to retrieve the prodigal pup. As the door opened, she found that Lucy was dripping wet. The neighbor laughed and explained: "I heard a lot of commotion, looked outside, and found Lucy swimming in my pool."

After thanking the kind man for his help, my sister brought Lucy home to dry off.

Our walk with God operates in a similar way—we enter seasons of fear or doubt, and the natural human instinct is to run. So, we run hard and fast away from Christ, intent on seeking answers and pleasure elsewhere. We're always looking for that fancy swimming pool.

In the Old Testament, Jonah tried to run, only to end up in worse circumstances, stuck in the belly of a big fish. Adam and Eve tried to hide from God after eating forbidden fruit. Running only delayed the inevitable, and no matter where they went, God always found them.

Adam, Eve, and Jonah remind us that we can't hide from our Lord. His compassionate nature is to seek us out, bring us home, dry our tears, and hold us close. Let's remember that God always seeks out those he loves.

Dear God, sometimes I want to run far away. I've messed up, disappointed you or others, and I don't measure up. Sometimes I run because I'm confused or lonely, but running away rarely solves my problems. Help me to understand that you love me deeply and that I'm never hidden from your care. Let me trust that your greatest pleasure is knowing that I'm safe in your arms. Please help me to stop running and hiding so that I come to you for healing and wholeness.

PAWS TO THINK

Why do you think we want to run from the God who created us and knows us better than we know ourselves?

DID YOU KNOW

A dog's shoulder blades are unattached from the rest of the skeleton to allow greater flexibility for running.

WILLING TO WAIT

Wait patiently for the LORD.
Be brave and courageous.
Yes, wait patiently for the LORD.

PSALM 27:14 NLT

Oh, please don't give me those sad eyes, BJ," his owner pleaded. "I know you'll miss me while I'm out, but I'll only be gone for two hours. When I come back, we can play with your stuffed squeaky toys. I don't want to leave you, but I have to run some errands. You'll be okay. I promise."

With those parting words from his owner, BJ turned around and waddled into his crate to curl up for a nice afternoon nap.

BJ is quite the character. He's a twenty-pound tri-color Shih Tzu who lives a charmed life. He owns a fluffy bed, although frequently he claims his owner's queen-size bed. His toy collection rivals that of any toddler, and he only has to bat his dark eyes and curl up in your lap to wiggle his way to another tasty treat. BJ is well-loved and pampered.

Out of all his traits, his patience shines the brightest.

Last year, BJ watched his human father move out of the house and into a special facility for people with dementia. He lost his primary walking partner. It was no easy adjustment, but it seemed his little soul understood that he couldn't take time off to grieve this change. His human mother needed an extra layer of love. Her husband of fifty years was declining, and she needed extra cuddles. No matter where she went, BJ always sat patiently in his crate or near the door, ready to jump into his momma's arms when the door opened.

When you stop and think about it, our God has the same character. No matter where we go or what we do, God always knows that we need his love. He longs to pour his compassion into our hearts and remind us that we are highly favored.

It was love that drove God's Son, Jesus Christ, to the cross, and it was love that kept him there despite the pain and rejection. It is love that keeps God by our side every day, even when we think we don't need him. Let's embrace our God who loves unconditionally.

Dear God, when I stop and think about how much you love me, I am humbled. You love me unconditionally, even when I'm at my worst. I want to learn to rest in your care for me. I want to always remember that you are sitting by the door, waiting for my return. Remind me to bask in your deep compassion. Help me tell others of your marvelous love.

PAWS TO THINK

Have you ever wondered why God is so patient with us, even in our moments of disobedience?

DID YOU KNOW

The Shih Tzu is originally from Tibet, and the name means "Little Lion."

DOGGiE DiVA

After licking his dinner bowl clean, Toy, a miniature dachshund, went to look for his owners. Mom was on the sofa and Dad was at the kitchen table. These two-legged servants were perfectly placed to address his still-present hunger, yet they did nothing! Toy picked up his bowl and sauntered over to the dog food cupboard. CLANG! The peaceful silence broke as the bowl hit the tile floor. Toy had spoken and was demanding a response.

Toy had developed a new game for his human servants. He called this game *Feed Me Now Before I Faint!* Toy knew that he was on a strict diet—a diet he didn't enjoy. There wasn't enough food in the bowl to satisfy and he was smart enough to know exactly where Mom and Dad kept his food supplies.

Knowing there was more, Toy tried to convince his

parents to yield to his demands. His usual tricks of sad eyes and soft whimpers hadn't worked. A higher level of persuasion was needed. His new plan involved loud noise and demanding eyes. Following every meal, Toy would carry his empty bowl to the cupboard, drop it on the floor, and sit at the feet of his owners until somebody moved. Minutes would pass, but the determined dachshund stayed put.

Unfortunately, I can be just as demanding with the Lord. "God, I want things done this way on this day!" I stomp my feet, huff and puff, and tell God he'd better do something before I lose my cool. Heaven stays silent, and God doesn't move. He doesn't fill the bowl again. He doesn't respond the way I think he should respond, and it hurts.

We must remember that his silence or lack of action is always part of a bigger plan, and he doesn't respond because the timing isn't right. What we want God to do could actually be the worst choice for us, so we must trust that inaction is his most compassionate action. Let's commit to approaching our God with dignity rather than demands, trusting that his ways are best.

Dear God, thank you for loving me in my impatience. I don't always know why you act the way you do. I pray that you will give me a sweet feeling of peace when you stay silent as I ask for things that aren't right for me. Teach me to wait. Teach me to seek. Teach me to take a deep breath and to avoid a demanding spirit that may be inconsistent with your desires for me. Let me find patience in your daily presence.

PAWS TO THINK

Why do we always want to rush God to act when the Scriptures tell us that his timing is rarely our timing?

DID YOU KNOW

Dogs are as smart as two-year-old children, meaning they understand roughly the same number of words and gestures as a toddler.

SANCTIFIED SOUL

Do nothing out of selfish ambition or vain conceit. Rather, in humility value others above yourselves, not looking to your own interests but each of you to the interests of the others.

PHILIPPIANS 2:3-4 NIV

Don't tell me he's in the bathtub again. What is his problem?" Rocky's owner, a high-energy mom who goes by M.J., couldn't believe that her sixty-pound golden retriever loved the bath so much. I mean, what dog really *loves* a bath? But Rocky was no ordinary dog. Rocky was a sanctified, revitalized, totally purified saint in the doggie kingdom.

Like most golden retrievers, Rocky loved outdoor walks and play sessions. His autumn roll in the leaves was followed by winter romps in the snow and spring naps in the mud. He would run, tumble, and play with the neighborhood pups, driving his owner to near exhaustion following an excursion.

Rocky hid one big secret from his neighborhood fur friends. While Rocky enjoyed traditional dirty dog pleasures, from mud puddles to swamp visits, he preferred cleanliness. Yes, that's right. Rocky willingly took himself to the bathtub on a regular basis to get cleaned up.

His penchant for cleanliness even manifested itself in his choice of toys, preferring the companionship of clean white socks from the laundry basket over plush toys. Rocky was living out the old saying, "Cleanliness is next to godliness." In Rocky's head, his cleanliness gave him higher status in the animal kingdom.

When I think about Rocky, I sometimes see myself, particularly when I reflect on my church behavior. While I try to be humble, the fact that I regularly attend church, put money in the offering plate, or sing solos in the choir fools me into thinking that I'm at a higher level, a completely purified and sanctified saint in the kingdom of believers.

Some days, I think I'm a Class-A Christian, looking down on those other worshippers who haven't bothered to climb into God's big bathtub to get their sin scrubbed away. I've decided that God loves me more because I look better, smell better, and am sanctified.

The reality is that God loves humility. God isn't looking for perfect, cleaned-up saints. He's looking for humble servant hearts.

Dear God, help me tackle my pride. Never let me go around believing that you love me or value me more than anyone else in your kingdom. Remind me that I am sanctified to be of service. My purification isn't designed to give me bragging rights at church or in the local community. May I always remain humble, kind, and patient with those around me, so I don't dishonor your name.

PAWS TO THINK

Do you think it hurts your testimony when you let your sanctification turn you into a pious and prideful believer? How can you choose to walk in humility?

DID YOU KNOW

Dogs and cats slurp water the same way.

PAWSITIVELY PROTECTED

You are my hiding place;
you will protect me from trouble
and surround me with songs of deliverance.

PSALM 32:7 NIV

"Grandma is missing. Grandma is *missing*!" Fear flooded John and Nancy's hearts at 2:00 a.m. Belle, their chocolate Labrador, had awakened them with excessive barking. While trying to calm her, they realized the door to Grandma's bedroom was open, meaning a sweet elderly lady with dementia was missing. Belle was barking for a reason.

As John ran upstairs and Nancy downstairs, Belle ran outside and barked even louder. When it was evident that Grandma was nowhere in the house, the family ran outdoors in a panic.

Grandma was frail, unstable, and susceptible to cold and illness due to her age and dementia. The last thing she needed was exposure to the winter elements. How had she made it past the locked door and down the rocky path from the house? Nothing made sense as the family frantically searched for her.

As the search expanded, Nancy caught sight of Belle running in furious circles. She ran toward of the furry tail, unsure of what she might find. As she drew closer, she saw Grandma, trapped in the middle of Belle's circle.

Belle's owners suddenly realized that the excessive barking was Belle's warning alarm that something was wrong. She had protected Grandma until reinforcements arrived. In that moment of heroic recovery, Belle exemplified the purest nature of our Great Shepherd.

Our God is a God of protection—a God who wants to keep us physically, emotionally, and spiritually safe. God gives us many warning signs that we often ignore, but he's still there to encircle us with deeper compassion when we choose to ignore the danger signs.

God knows the greatest safety is the Word and his wisdom. He wants to protect and provide to grow our hearts, minds, and souls, but we must be willing to trust him.

Dear God, please protect me today. Hold me tight and teach me to desire what you desire for my life. Do not let me fall into a dangerous place of disobedience or irreverence. Instead, encircle me with a compassionate love that keeps Satan's threats at bay. Remind me of your love for your creation, and that you will do anything possible to keep me in a safe place. Put people and purposes in my life that let me thrive, and never let me stray far from your loving embrace.

PAWS TO THINK

Wouldn't life be easier at times if we trusted that God always wants to keep us close and safe?

DID YOU KNOW

Dogs and humans both experience rapid eye movement (REM) sleep stages that typically encourage dreaming. The twitching and paw movements that occur during sleep are signs that your dog is dreaming.

TOP DOG

The wisdom from above is first of all pure.
It is also peace loving, gentle at all times,
and willing to yield to others.
It is full of mercy and the fruit of good deeds.
It shows no favoritism and is always sincere.

JAMES 3:17 NLT

Our two mini schnauzers genuinely love each other and get along. However, when it comes to who gets to lay between us in bed, our female Zoe always get that coveted position. She is never willing to let our male, Rocky, be the top dog.

She sometimes deploys distraction tactics by pulling out a toy. While Rocky's busy playing, she jumps up on our bed and secures her spot. Rocky is then obliged to lay by our feet while she happily gets extra tummy rubs. Thankfully, he doesn't seem to mind his dominant sister constantly vying for our complete attention, but sometimes we intentionally force Zoe to give Rocky the spotlight.

Isn't it easy to be focused on ourselves? We too desire

to be in the best position possible. We sometimes distract or manipulate others for our own agendas. We justify our actions by rationalizing we're making the right decision even if we sideline someone else in the process. Being right doesn't make us wise.

In today's verse, James explains that godly wisdom stems from pure motives. It is gentle and willing to yield for the betterment of someone else. A Christian speaker once shared she'd always loved being a Sunday school teacher, but as she began to travel more frequently for speaking engagements, she realized she could no longer do both well. When she stepped down from teaching the class, a younger woman took over and the group continued to thrive. The new leader brought along her own life experiences and a different style of teaching that breathed new life into the class.

If our ultimate goal is to bring God glory in everything we do, our focus will shift from us to others. Willingness to put aside our own plans doesn't come naturally to us, so we must allow the Holy Spirit to work within us. Then we can see others the way God does—without favoritism.

Father, examine my heart and help me make decisions with the right motives. It's so easy to become self-absorbed and make choices with only my benefits in mind. Help my desire to be wise trump my desire to be right. Guide me to opportunities in which I can yield my own ideas and agendas for the good of someone else. Thank you for the example Christ left us when he willingly set aside his glory to serve those around him. Please help me to do likewise.

PAWS TO THINK

When in charge of an event or project, how willing are you to implement others' ideas if it means deviating from your original plan?

DID YOU KNOW

When your dog licks you,
it releases endorphins,
gives them a sense of satisfaction,
and relieves stress.

FEELING INADEQUATE

That the man of God may be complete,
equipped for every good work.

2 Timothy 3:17 esv

"Come on, Felix. You can do it!" I called to my cocker spaniel puppy as he whined at the top of the stairs, hopefully waiting for someone to carry him down. Felix's long ears and short legs made walking down the stairs awkward, and he was frightened to try.

However, after continued verbal encouragement and the promise of a tasty reward, Felix decided to trust the confidence in my voice and take that first step. At first, he wobbled and stumbled a bit, but after a few days he was able to go up and down the stairs with ease.

Have you ever felt like Felix, trapped at the top of the stairs and not ready for something God has called you to do? Maybe you've thought, *I'm not good enough, I'm not strong enough, I'm not ready for this.* In the New Testament, we find Paul asking God on three separate occasions to deliver him from what Paul called a thorn in the flesh.

Whatever the affliction, Paul felt it hindered him from completing the physical and mental demands required in his ministry. However, God showed Paul that it was his weakness that best equipped him to complete God's call on his life. Where Paul was weak, he had to rely on God's strength.

Our inadequacies keep us dependent on God. Like Felix, we stumble and bumble a bit, but weakness teaches us to rely on his strength to get us through. We have to acknowledge our inability and shift our dependency to God. The moment we realize that we can't go on alone, we receive the strength we need. God's timing rarely aligns with ours, but we can trust that if he is calling us to do something, He will equip us to complete the task.

> Lord, do not let my inadequacies keep me from fulfilling the things you've called me to do. It's so easy to become overwhelmed when I find myself in situations I feel unequipped to deal with. Sometimes, I pray that you would take away my weaknesses instead of letting you use me to reflect your strength in my life. Thank you for showing me how you equipped Moses and Paul to carry out the things you entrusted them to do. Help me—like them—to choose to trust you in the middle of my fears.

PAWS TO THINK

When you are put into a situation that makes you uncomfortable, is it up to you to muster the strength to figure out a solution? Or do you trust that God will equip you to complete the task and look to his Word for strength?

DID YOU KNOW

Three dogs survived the sinking of the Titanic—two Pomeranians and one Pekingese.

USING OUR GIFTS

Having gifts that differ according to the grace given to us,
let us use them.

ROMANS 12:6 ESV

I was playing catch on the front lawn with my two grand-kids, enjoying the brisk fall air. My black Lab, Lady, was out front with us, desperately trying to get my atten-tion. I could tell she was getting frustrated when I didn't acknowledge her lively barking.

All of a sudden, Lady ran into the wooded area beside the driveway, hauled over a large tree branch, and tried to engage me in a playful game of tug-of-war. That smart dog realized that the grandkids and I were playing together and wanted in on the fun, too. I guess she grew insecure when all attention was on the kids, and she felt a little neglected.

We sometimes doubt our worth to our heavenly mas-ter, too. We compare the spiritual gifts God has chosen to give someone else with the ones he's entrusted to us. This is especially easy to do when our abilities may not get the attention or accolades we hoped they would. We question if our spiritual gift is significant or if it adds any value to the body of Christ.

Rest assured, it does. The human body, created in the image of God, is truly a masterpiece. Some parts of the body are visible, like the eyes and mouth, but unseen parts like the heart and brain enable the visible parts to function. Similarly, some spiritual aptitudes, like teaching, are more noticeable within the church. Equally as important is the person who has the gift of hospitality and readily opens up her home to encourage someone who might be hurting. Also important is the person with the gift of administration, who keeps track of the church's finances.

Our spiritual gifts are meant to benefit body of Christ. Every gift is needed to minister to the world, and each offers a unique contribution. Let's commit to fully using the abilities and talents God has given us, knowing that our gifts will be effective for his work.

Father, help me to be grateful for the spiritual gifts you have entrusted to me. Help me to strike a healthy balance of humility with my value as a person created in your image. You want to use me to strengthen the body of Christ. Help me to see that the gifts you've given me are as important as the gifts you've given others. Remind me that my spiritual gifts are fruits of the Spirit.

PAWS TO THINK

Why do we associate the spiritual gifts that are more visible as being more important?

DID YOU KNOW

According to the American Kennel Club, the Labrador retriever has made their Top 10 Most Popular Breeds list for the past twenty-five years, which is longer than any other breed.

THE PUPARAZZI

My dear brothers and sisters, how can you claim to have faith in our glorious Lord Jesus Christ if you favor some people over others?

JAMES 2:1 NLT

After my brain surgery, I dreaded going out in public. My hair was cut very short, and in some parts, it was completely shaved. I had a large incision that started at the top of my skull and ran all the way down to the base of my neck, like a zipper. I knew I made people feel uncomfortable, and they avoided making eye contact with me.

My two mini schnauzers, however, seemed unaffected by my physical changes. I could still hear them excitedly barking and see their bearded faces peering through the front windows when my car pulled into the driveway. I lovingly nicknamed them my own personal puparazzi because they acted like I was a celebrity—a person of importance.

What if we treated others with the same openness and love that our dogs shower on us despite our looks, economic status, or size? We are wide off the mark when we allow our personal prejudices to determine how we act toward others. We need to be intentional in our interactions with others. We can look for those we can demonstrate the love of God to especially when we're tempted to ignore someone because we would step out of our comfort zones.

We must guard against showing favor to a select few while disregarding others. We should ask God to make us aware when we do treat someone poorly. The glory of the Gospel is that it's available and freely given to all. Scripture tells us that all of heaven rejoices over one repentant sinner. It is our faith in Christ, not our background or status, that ushers us into the family of God. No distinction is made because we are each created in the image of God.

Focusing on God's glory levels the playing field and helps us treat one another with the same grace and mercy we've lavishly received. Let's follow the example of our furry friends and treat all we encounter as the beloved and valued people they are.

Lord, I confess there are times I have allowed my own petty distinctions to affect the way I treat others. Remind me that each person is created in your image and holds intrinsic value. Thank you for offering your grace and mercy freely to me, with no conditions or strings. Give me a renewed heart, so I can be on the lookout for those I can love in your name. Thank you for my pets who unconditionally love and affirm me, even on days when I mess up or don't deserve it.

PAWS TO THINK

Why is it easy to allow our own personal prejudices to determine how we treat others?

DID YOU KNOW

For his Shetland sheepdog, Paul McCartney recorded an ultrasonic whistle only audible to dogs at the end of the Beatles' song "A Day in the Life."

WALK WITH ME

I can never escape from your Spirit!
I can never get away from your presence!

PSALM 139:7 NLT

Our daughter, Emily, had her first seizure when she was five years old. It was scary not knowing when she would have another one, especially at night. We got her a seizure-alert service dog named Cody. Cody had the uncanny ability of sensing when Emily was going to have a seizure and would alert us by walking protectively around Emily and barking.

It's not completely understood how seizure-alert dogs are able to sense an upcoming seizure, but it is clear that they have an intimate understanding of their owners. They are quick to raise alarm when needed.

All of us have a deep desire to be intimately known. We want to know that we have someone looking out for us, like Cody looked out for Emily. We want to turn to someone with our hurts and fears.

Jesus promises to never leave us nor forsake us. We can't

physically see him, but through faith, we can trust that the God who counts the hairs of our heads and watches every sparrow fall isn't observing us from a distance. He is walking right beside us.

Our God is omniscient, meaning he has complete knowledge of all things. He knows our most intimate needs and desires. He is also omnipresent, so there is nowhere we can go where he is not with us. Where we are limited by our humanity, we have access to a God who has no limits, and whose presence nothing else can replace.

Knowing Cody kept a constant and vigilant watch over Emily eased our constant state of worry and allowed Emily to maintain a healthy level of independence into her teen years. Today, we know our faithful God will complete the work he's begun in our lives and give us the confidence to press forward. We know his perfect love will sustain us, no matter what scary circumstances we encounter.

Lord, only when I'm resting in your perfect love can I let go of my many fears. Thank you for being an intimate God who invites his people into a deep and personal relationship. Help me to trust you when I face circumstances where it's hard to see your hand at work. As I go from situation to situation, may I depend on you for my strength, knowing with confidence that you will be there to help me through each and every one.

PAWS TO THiNK

Why is it hard to believe that God is right there with you when you are going through something difficult?

DiD YOU KNOW

Helen Keller was the first person to bring an Akita dog to the United States. She was gifted one by the Japanese government on a trip to Japan.

GUARD YOUR HEART

Guard your heart above all else,
for it determines the course of your life.

PROVERBS 4:23 NLT

I decided it was time to test our one-year-old miniature dachshund, Pepper. Instead of putting him in his crate, I allowed him to roam freely around the house while I went grocery shopping. He'd had no potty accidents for several months, and I assumed he'd curl up in the oversized arm chair by the front window and wait patiently for my return.

I couldn't have been more wrong. As I walked in the front door, arms full of groceries, the smell that assaulted my nostrils was a clear indication that Pepper had broken his accident-free streak. Garbage from our bathroom trash can was strewn across the living room floor. Upset as I was, my heart sank I called for Pepper and he didn't appear. I found him looking quite pitiful in our master bedroom. His collar was caught on the dresser knob he'd been gnawing.

As I freed Pepper from the unexpected prison he'd made for himself, I thought about how we can imprison ourselves when we leave our hearts unguarded. It's easy to neglect our quiet time with God, not maintain a vibrant prayer life, and not prioritize gathering with other believers. We convince ourselves that we're spiritually mature enough, leaving ourselves wide open to the seemingly endless traps of this world.

It's not enough to want to do what's right. We must proactively guard our hearts, so we can protect ourselves from a root of bitterness that can destroy relationships. We must guard our tongues, knowing the weight our words carry.

Once Pepper was free, his little tail began to wag. He happily followed me around as I cleaned up his messes. Our heavenly Father is also quick to untangle the mess we've made, and we once again follow him. What a comfort for when our hearts go astray!

Father, it's easy to think I can handle things on my own or convince myself I have it all together. When I forget to guard my heart, I go off-course and sometimes find myself in a self-made prison. Please forgive me for the times I don't make my relationship with you the priority it should be. I invite you, like King David did, to search my heart and renew a right spirit within me. Thank you for your grace and mercy that lovingly guides me back when I lose my way.

PAWS TO THINK

Have you ever done something completely out of character and then questioned why you allowed yourself to do that? What can you do to change that?

DID YOU KNOW

Dogs' whiskers can pick up subtle changes in air currents, allowing them to discern the size, shape, and speed of nearby objects.

IMITATING THE MASTER

Imitate God, therefore, in everything you do,
because you are his dear children.

EPHESIANS 5:1 NLT

My husband and I were enjoying the colorful foliage of a crisp fall day as we leisurely strolled through Central Park. We stopped to watch a man who was training his golden retriever. The dog's name was Charlie. Without any verbal commands, Charlie imitated whatever his master was doing.

We were impressed as Charlie seemingly mimicked even his owner's facial expressions. You could almost hear Charlie say, "No!" as he turned his head from side to side or feel his frustration when he dropped his head against his chest and looked down.

When Charlie's owner was satisfied with his performance, the dog was rewarded with vigorous pats on the head and lots of verbal praise. Charlie relished attention because pleasing his master had been the motivating force.

As we continued to walk, I kept seeing Charlie's face. Like Charlie, do we imitate Christ, our master? Do others look at our lives and see glimpses of God's love and grace through our actions?

Some aspects of God's character are easy to emulate, like loving those that openly embrace and appreciate us. It gets much harder to do those things for people who've hurt or wronged us, and yet that's the example Christ left us to follow. When the religious group of Jesus's day questioned his choice to eat and drink with a group notorious for rampant sin, Jesus reminded them that it's not healthy people that need a physician but the sick.

We can't imitate Christ by our own strength or need for human applause and validation. The key is that our motivation should be to please our master. As we draw closer to our heavenly Father, our desires start to shift. We begin to truly long for those around us to experience the grace we have received. Just as Charlie imitated his owner because he belonged to him, we are to imitate Christ. As daughters of the King, we belong to him.

Lord, as your dear child, I am commanded to imitate the grace and mercy I've received to others. I know I have to rely on the Holy Spirit within me to accomplish this. In my own strength, I could never imitate your characteristics. Thank you for Christ's example, which gives me a pattern to follow. Thank you for inviting me to come boldly before your throne of grace, knowing you will give me exactly what I need as I strive to be more like you.

PAWS TO THINK

What daily things should we be doing in order to ensure our thoughts and words are accurate reflections of God's love?

DID YOU KNOW

Laika, a stray dog found on the streets of Moscow, was the first animal to orbit earth on the Soviet space craft Sputnik 2.

THE RiGHT MOMENT

"Who knows but that you have come to your royal position
for such a time as this?"

ESTHER 4:14 NIV

My two-year old daughter and I were splashing around
our backyard pool when our rumbling stomachs indicated
it was time for lunch. I walked and hurriedly put down
my daughter and the other items I was carrying. I didn't
ensure that the back door had shut securely behind me. As
I buttered some bread for grilled cheese sandwiches, my
daughter silently slipped out the back door and headed
straight for the pool.

When my brown Labrador, Dixie, began wildly barking,
I looked out the window over our kitchen sink. My heart
turned to lead when I saw my daughter floating face down
in the pool. I ran to frantically pull her from the water, and
I was overcome with relief as she coughed and spit up the
water she'd swallowed.

After I had calmed down, I was filled with immense
gratitude for Dixie. If she hadn't raised the alarm, this

terrible situation could have ended in tragedy. Dixie was in the right place at the right time.

In today's verse, Esther was in the right place and time to be crowned queen. God orchestrated events so she would be in the palace at just the right time to petition the king, saving her Jewish people from annihilation.

We, too, have been divinely appointed by God in our current positions, be they as mothers, wives, co-workers, or friends. We carry our own spheres of vital influence, though we may perceive them as inconsequential. Before the foundations of the world, God knew us and ordained our days.

Like Esther, we have a choice. We can trust God and allow him to work through us, achieving his purpose for our lives. Or, we can choose to walk in disobedience and allow our fears and doubts to prevent us from accomplishing his will. Our lives are part of his greater plan, and knowing that gives courage when our current situations or circumstances become difficult. We can choose to live with ease, or we can ask God for the boldness to live with eternal significance.

Lord, sometimes I question why I'm in my current situation. It can feel like my present roles are insignificant. Help me to remember that nothing in my life happens by accident. Your Word tells me that all of my days are before you. In your divine wisdom, you have placed me in the best position to accomplish the unique purposes you've intended. Give me courage to set aside my own will and desires and to instead follow your leadership. Only by obeying you will I find lasting joy.

PAWS TO THINK

Have you gone through a difficult situation that you couldn't understand at the time, but you can now see God's purpose in allowing it?

DID YOU KNOW

More than half of all U.S. presidents have owned dogs.

ALL EYES ON ME

The LORD said to Samuel, "Do not look on his appearance
or on the height of his stature, because I have rejected him.
For the LORD sees not as man sees: man looks on the outward
appearance, but the LORD looks on the heart."

1 SAMUEL 16:7 ESV

We've tried to discourage our Alaskan malamute, Max,
from begging at the kitchen table. He's tall enough that
he can steal food from the kitchen counter. We've worked
hard to dissuade this type of behavior, so we never take
food from our plates and give it directly to Max. However,
that hasn't deterred him from trying to sneak food when
our backs are turned.

One night, my husband grilled some steaks, and in my
peripheral vision I could see Max moving closer and closer
to the table. When I turned to scold him, he looked away,
shifting his gaze straight ahead. As soon as I went back
to eating my dinner, Max inched a little bit closer. When
I turned to look at him for the second time, he swiftly

looked behind him, trying to convince me he wasn't aiming for a piece of my steak.

We sometimes act sneakily, too. We behave a certain way when we know we're being observed or when we want to be noticed. Then, we act a differently when we think no one's looking. We fool others into thinking we are perfect, but we can't dupe God. What is truly in our hearts will eventually manifest itself through our actions.

The prophet Nathan was perplexed when God had sent him to anoint one of Jesse's sons as the next king of Israel. None of the sons that Nathan thought would be the one were chosen. Instead, God chose Jesse's youngest son, David, to be king. Nathan was only able to see the men's external qualities, but God was able to discern their hearts.

Who we are when no one else is around is who we truly are. If we are not privately spending time in prayer and in the Word, then we will not exhibit genuine fruits of the Spirit. Just as Max wasn't able to fool me by looking away, neither can we fool God about what is motivating us.

Father, I am quick to put my best foot forward when I know others are watching me, then behave differently when I think I'm alone. Forgive me for the times I feign concern or deceive someone else for the benefit of puffing myself up. You see what is in my heart. Transform my selfish motives, so that any good deeds I do will bring you glory. Humble my heart and make it willing to do your work.

PAWS TO THINK

Why is it easier to worry about the reception of our external actions than to be concerned about our thoughts and attitudes?

DID YOU KNOW

Dogs often curl up in balls when they sleep, following age-old instincts to keep warm and protect their vital organs.

GIVE THE DOG A BONE

Hear my cry, O God, listen to my prayer;
from the end of the earth I call to you when my heart is faint.
Lead me to the rock that is higher than I.

PSALM 61:1-2 ESV

Shadow was crouched in a corner of the shelter, which hinted that he'd experienced a rough beginning. One of the shelter workers shared with us that the black Lab's original owners had been abusive, and they surrendered him before he was a year old.

When we first brought Shadow home, he was understandably apprehensive. We would often reward him with milk bones when he let us pet him or decided to approach us of his own accord. Shadow's fears quickly began to dissipate, replaced with the energy of a thriving puppy. Shadow was great with our kids, and despite being cruelly treated, he was completely trusting. He didn't let the difficult circumstances of his past prevent him from enjoying his new life.

Life is often frustrating and overwhelming, and we can get cynical. We are left with scars that prevent us from moving forward and living the abundant life God intended for us. Like Shadow, we end up internally cowering, emotions numbed as we go through the motions of life.

However, God beckons us closer. He promises that only he can bring beauty from our ashes, restoring the years that the locusts of life have eaten. In our anguish, we must seek the lifeline of our God. We must allow him to lead us out of the debris. We can cling to him as our rock.

Shadow didn't allow his initial mistreatment to prevent him from embracing his new and loving family, and neither should we. We are overcomers because our souls are safe in Christ. We can trust he'll bring healing and surround us with his abiding joy. He treats our wounds with the power of his Word.

We can view our circumstances from the valley we're currently in, or we can allow our awareness of God to shift our focus to the rock that promises us a place of refuge.

Father, life is messy, and I can easily become jaded. I wonder if anything good can come from what I'm going through. Help me to cling to the promises in your Word instead of my emotions. I often feel I have to solve my problems in my own strength. Remind me that when my heart becomes overwhelmed, I must fully cling to you—my rock. Thank you that there is no situation that's hopeless or beyond your ability to use for my good.

PAWS TO THINK

Do you immediately run to God when
faced with a difficult situation,
or is your initial reaction to try to fix
things on your own?

DID YOU KNOW

The first commercially prepared dog food was introduced in 1860 by an English businessman named James Spratt. Spratt's dog biscuit was a mix of wheat meal, vegetables, beetroot, and beef blood.

NEVER FAR

"My Presence will go with you, and I will give you rest."

Exodus 33:14 NIV

In our house, I was always the one who pushed to get a pet. My husband wasn't hostile to the idea, but he wasn't the instigator. One day, we became the proud owners of Sadie Mae, a tiny rescue Yorkie. She was a beautiful dog, but she'd had a rough life as the product of a puppy mill. Even though I was the one who had insisted on getting her, it was my husband who won her heart.

My husband works out of an office in our home, and Sadie Mae immediately took up residence on a pillow near his desk. No amount of coaxing could lure her to my side.

Six weeks after we got her, my husband had a bad fall, shattering every bone in his face. This mishap led to several surgeries and a long recovery at home. Because he couldn't navigate the stairs at first, we made a bed for him in the family room. We tucked a twin-size bed into the corner and this allowed him to be part of all our holiday festivities. It also made it easier for me to keep an eye on him.

I had a helper in the nursing department. Sadie Mae shared that duty with joy and dedication. It was almost impossible to pry her away from him. He spent a lot of time sleeping. Because of the pain, it wasn't always a peaceful rest. He tossed and turned, shifting frequently as he searched for a way to get comfortable. Instead of running away, Sadie Mae found place on his bed where she wouldn't get crushed, but my husband could still reach her.

Her dedication gave me a picture of what God's constant care really looks like. We don't see how closely God stays with us. We're preoccupied with the pain of life and don't notice his loving attention. Even when we're miserable and lashing out, he's never far away.

Just like tiny Sadie Mae, God can't be driven away. He is dedicated to his precious children. His love is constant, and his comfort is immediate.

Dear Lord, sometimes life leaves me flat on my back, but you arrange circumstances to get me through tough times. Thank you for never leaving me. You are always there, no matter what circumstances I face. Even when life takes a sudden turn, I can count on you. Remind me of your close presence when I am wrapped up in my circumstances. Help me to remember to reach out my hand in faith, knowing you are always close to my side.

PAWS TO THINK

Have you reached out to God lately?
Give it a try and see how close he truly is.

DID YOU KNOW

One of the first therapy dogs on record was a Yorkshire terrier named Smokey.

FELLOWSHIP

"Where two or three gather together as my followers,
I am there among them."

MATTHEW 18:20 NLT

My husband and I have a morning routine. After we get up and settle in with our coffee, we take time to pray together. When we began caring for our son's dog, the pup insisted on joining our morning prayer time.

It began when he was just a puppy. To make sure he stayed out of mischief while we were otherwise occupied, we kept him with us during our morning devotion time. For him, it wasn't enough to be nearby. He wanted to be right up in the middle of things. Our new morning routine began.

Now, even if Cosmo is just back for a weekend visit, he looks forward to our time together. All it takes is, "Are you ready to pray?" and Cosmo comes running. He's not content to sit at our feet. He scrambles up and sits with his head on our clasped hands. He's most happy when he's nestled in between us. This sweet addition to our time of fellowship has become a precious part of starting our day.

I know that God is using this precocious pup to teach us about the fellowship of prayer. God's attitude toward prayer is a lot like Cosmo's. He isn't content to hover around the edges while we pour out a laundry list of wants and needs. Instead, he's intimately involved in the process. He's in our midst, touching us, reminding us of how much he loves us.

This consistent, intimate time spent with Cosmo has strengthened our bond with him. Likewise, regular meetings with God strengthen our relationship with him. God wants to be involved in every aspect of our lives.

> Dear Lord, what a gift it is that you want to spend time with your children. Though all of creation needs you, you always have time for me. Don't let me take this gift for granted. Instead, help me to desire more of you every moment of every day. I hate to admit it, but it's easy to get busy and forget our daily time together. Keep my priorities in line, and don't let me drift out of the habit of meeting with you.

PAWS TO THINK

What can you do today to invite God to
be more intimately involved in your life?

DID YOU KNOW

*There are more than a dozen separate muscles
that control a dog's ear movements. This is what
makes a dog's ears so expressive.*

RESCUE ME

"The Son of Man has come to seek and to save
that which was lost."

LUKE 19:10 NASB

It was a cold winter day, but my son insisted it was a great day for a hike. As he and a friend made their way around a local lake, movement on a small island close to shore caught his eye. He looked closely and realized it was a puppy.

Knowing the size of my son's heart, I wasn't surprised by his quick decision. He bent down and removed his shoes and socks. While his friend watched, he waded into the icy water. He wasn't daunted by the obstacles. The only thing on his mind was rescuing that precious dog.

When he clambered up onto the dry land of the island, the puppy whimpered and backed away, unsure of his rescuer's intent. His fur was covered with mud, and the stark outline of his ribs showed that he hadn't eaten regularly for some time. My son squatted down and spoke softly. "Come on, boy. I'm here to help."

The puppy hesitated for a long moment. Then, instead of slowly moving toward his rescuer, he took a running leap of faith and launched himself into my son's arms. That moment sealed their hearts together. They've been constant companions ever since.

I can't think about this wonderful event without tearing up. Not only is it a beautiful story of my son and his dog, but it's a perfect picture of what God does for each of us. Our heavenly Father never leaves us stranded. When we're alone and lost, he comes after us, tackling every obstacle. The world has abandoned us and left us to starve, but God never will. His love seeks us out and rescues us from a life of isolation and fear.

Dear Lord, it amazes me how much you love me. The fact that you would search me out and rescue me to be part of your family leaves me breathless. Thank you for coming after me. Even now, when I drift away, you're quick to draw me back to your side. Don't let me forget the sacrifice you made for me. Put markers in my life that remind me of how much you care. When life gets difficult, knowing how much you love me sustains me.

PAWS TO THINK

Looking back on your life, consider all the
ways God has rescued you.

DID YOU KNOW

*Puppies grow to half their body weight in the
first four to five months.*

REMOVING TANGLES

Everyone has sinned;
we all fall short of God's glorious standard.

ROMANS 3:23 NLT

Some dogs need more grooming than others, and some of us love the extra effort required. Sadie Mae was one of those high-maintenance pups. She was a gorgeous Yorkie with a long flowing coat. Yes, I could have kept her coat short, but I loved the way she looked with her silky hair.

She was a sight to see. Taking her on walks tended to stop traffic—almost everyone had a comment about how beautiful she was, and many wanted a chance to pet her. She adored the attention. After a bath and blow dry she loved to parade around the house, head held high.

What she didn't like was the tangles that appeared within a few days. No matter how often I brushed her, that long hair insisted on tying itself into knots. The knottier she got, the more Sadie Mae ducked and dodged visibility.

Perhaps part of it was she knew when her coat wasn't its best, and she felt ashamed. The main issue was that she knew I would remove those tangles, and the process wasn't always pleasant. To make sure the knots stayed manageable, I made it part of our nightly routine to comb out her hair. I did my best to keep her comfortable. I would settle her in my lap and slowly work through each snarl, cutting away any parts that were too tangled to comb. It was tedious work, and we were both glad when she was once again tangle-free.

I act the same way with God. When sin entangles me, I dread the process of removing it from my life. The more obvious it is, the more shame I feel. Truthfully, it's always easier when I make self-examination a regular part of my prayer time. God's removal of sin isn't meant to hurt us. He does his best to lead us gently through the process, and he never leaves us to handle it alone.

Dear Lord, I'm so weak. I hate getting tangled in sin. It slips into my life when I least expect it and ties me up in knots. When that happens, my first reaction is to hide and try to deal with it on my own. I know that doesn't work. It's only when I come to you for help that things get straightened out. Thank you for always willingly working through my struggles with me.

PAWS TO THINK

Consider the tangles of sin in your life.
Have you spent time with God lately,
so he can comb through those
troubling issues?

DID YOU KNOW

*Yorkshire terriers don't shed. They rely on their
owners to keep their coats looking sleek.*

ALWAYS FOUND

"I myself will search and find my sheep."

EZEKIEL 34:11 NLT

One of the hardest times for our family was a house move that forced us to find a new home for our dog. We couldn't find a place to rent that allowed a pet, so we had no choice. Fortunately, a close friend also faced a difficult move. She was a single mom with two children who needed a dog. We sent our dog to them with tears in our eyes, but we knew he was going to a family who would love him as much as we did.

It was incredibly hard to give up that furry part of our family. It was only knowing that he would be loved by my friend and her children that made it possible.

Fast forward a few months, and my friend called. She had an incredible story about the blessing this hand-me-down dog had turned out to be. Between the divorce and recent move, her oldest child had been struggling with depression. Her daughter hid her growing feelings of despair and had almost succeeded in fooling her family.

One evening, she disappeared after supper. As the seconds turned to minutes, fear seeped into her mother's heart. No one said it, but everyone feared the worst.

The dog stood by the back door, howling and whining louder with each minute that passed. Finally, they opened the door and let him out. He made a beeline toward a tiny shed on the edge of their property. With the dog jumping at the door, they opened it and found the child slumped on the floor, a bottle of pills beside her. At the hospital, the doctors pumped her stomach and made sure she got the help she needed. Thanks to the dog, they had found her in time.

God knows what lies ahead of us. He plans in advance and his help is never too late. He doesn't lose sight of us, and we're never far from his tender care. We cannot hide from him or slip through his fingers.

God knew what was coming and had everything in place to save my friend's daughter. He does that for each of us. He will always find us, even when despair tries to pull us under.

Dear Lord, you always know where I am. Even when I'm not aware of your presence, you're with me. Don't let me give in to despair. Wrap your love around me and hold me close. Put other people in my life to remind me how much you love me. Depression and sadness lead me to a place where all I want to do is give up. Help me find a community that reminds me of your constant presence.

PAWS TO THINK

How has God put things in place to help
you before you knew the assistance
would be needed?

DID YOU KNOW

*Dogs' noses are always wet because they secrete
a thin layer of mucous to help them absorb
scent. They then lick their noses to sample the
scent through their mouth.*

DISTRACTED CONSEQUENCES

Let your eyes look straight ahead;
fix your gaze directly before you.
Give careful thought to the paths for your feet
and be steadfast in all your ways.

PROVERBS 4:25-26 NIV

It seemed like a fun idea. Our son tied Jake's leash to his scooter to get the kind of speed he couldn't achieve under his own power. What could possibly go wrong?

The experiment got off to a strong start. Jimmy had positioned his scooter at the top of the hill, carefully placing Jake in front. At the bottom was our yard. The green grass was lush in the hot summer sun, and it was the perfect landing pad.

Off they went, and the scooter rushed down the hill, faster and faster. Then the unthinkable happened—a squirrel darted in front of Jake. Jimmy held on for dear life as the dog took a sharp left to follow the furry-tailed rodent.

The speeding scooter hit the curb and our son went one

way and his dog went the other. I rushed outside to pick up the pieces and comfort the fallen.

I saw that our son was fine, but Jake and the scooter were wrapped tightly around the tree, tied up by the leash. As I unwound the restraints, Jake whined and shot me a guilty look. I helped Jake inside and gave him a treat and some water, pondering the obvious lessons in the situation.

All too often, I find myself in a similar situation. I make plans and rush ahead without thinking it through. Like Jake, I have the best intentions, but I am easily distracted and unable to stay focused when the squirrels of life cross my path.

No matter what, God is always there to rescue me. He is watching, allowing me to make mistakes that will teach me valuable lessons. He doesn't leave me tied up in consequences, though. Instead, he picks up the pieces and shows me how much he loves me.

Dear Lord, sometimes it's hard for me to stay focused. I have the best intentions, but I'm easily distracted. Please help me to stay focused on the path you've set before me. I know there will come times when I stumble and fall. Don't let me get tangled up, even when it's my fault. Instead, protect me from those consequences and teach me to keep my eyes firmly fixed on you. Only when I stay close to you can I stay on track.

PAWS TO THINK

When things fall apart, do you remember to look up and let God pick up the pieces? How has that choice affected you?

DID YOU KNOW

In 2017, a total of about 89.7 million dogs lived in households in the United States.

HOLD MY HAND

The LORD makes firm the steps of the one who delights in him;
though he may stumble, he will not fall,
for the LORD upholds him with his hand.

PSALM 37:23-24 NIV

I love the way our oldest son learned how to walk. Like every other toddler, he began his journey by pulling up on anything his chubby little fists could lock onto. One day, the thing closest to him was Sherlock, our blond cocker spaniel.

I left our young son watching a video just long enough to return a glass to the kitchen. In those few seconds, he crawled to where our dog was standing. Before I could call out, Jimmy curled his small hands into the dog's fur and pulled himself into a standing position.

As he swayed beside our family pet, I froze, afraid that if I moved, the dog would take off and Jimmy would fall. As I eased toward them, Sherlock glanced at me, then fixed his concentration on the tiny figure using him for balance.

Before I could reach them, the dog took steps—literally.

He took a small step, just far enough so Jimmy had to take a step to stay upright. Slowly, they made their way across the floor, the dog taking one step at a time and my toddler learning how to walk.

I'd love to say I taught my son to walk, but in truth, it was our dog who patiently matched his doggy steps to the tiny toddler in his care. He was our son's shepherd, teaching him and keeping him safe.

It is a perfect picture of how God shepherds us. He's always there with us, matching our progress and staying close to give us the support we need. He knows when to nudge us forward and when to wait and let us take the next step alone.

God wants us to grow out of babyhood and learn to walk. He does not ask us to walk away from him. Instead, he wants to stay with us as he guides us, encourages us, and watches over us with limitless love and care.

Dear Lord, thank you for your infinite patience and care. I don't always notice how carefully you match your steps to mine. Help me to be more aware of the ways you support and love me. You're always there when I reach out to you. I never need to fear anything when I hold tightly to you. All the things I've accomplished have only come about because of your help. Don't let me wander away from you. Stick close to me, and never let me fall.

PAWS TO THINK

How has God guided your steps and helped you learn how to walk?

DID YOU KNOW

Human blood pressure goes down when petting a dog—and so does the dog's.

WHEN NO IS BEST

Don't turn your back on wisdom, for she will protect you.
Love her, and she will guard you.

PROVERBS 4:6 NLT

We'd only had Samantha a few months when our middle son was born. She immediately assigned herself as his doggy protector. As he began to crawl, and then walk, it quickly became a full-time job—one I would have been hard-pressed to handle alone.

We lived in a two-story house. The stairs from the second floor ended in our entry way at a solid slab of marble. Our toddler was fascinated with those stairs, and I was so afraid he'd climb up and fall—landing with devastating consequences on that hard floor.

One morning, I'd left both boys on the sofa watching cartoons while I got dressed. I'd just pulled on my jeans when I heard a blood-curdling scream from our toddler. Immediately, I thought of the gate and realized I'd neglected to put it up at the bottom of the stairs. My older son hollered at me to "come quick."

I raced to the front room, certain I'd find our youngest in a pool of gore. Instead, what I saw stopped me in my tracks. Standing across the opening of the stairs stood Samantha, blocking access to our toddler. He stood, red-faced and screaming, with both hands yanking at her fur. He was so mad he'd already pulled out several hunks, but she hadn't budged.

I rushed in and untangled the baby's fingers from her coat, but the dog didn't move until after I secured the child gate. I distracted my son and got him settled, then went to see Samantha. She had some bald patches but wasn't hurt. Our oldest son was petting her and telling her she was a good dog.

God also protects us from the consequences of poor choices. Often, we want something so badly that we don't see the danger that lies before us. Like my son, we just want our way. God loves us enough to tell us no—not because he wants to ruin our plans, but because he loves us and knows what's best for us.

Dear Lord, forgive me for being blind to your protection. I get so caught up in what I want that I forget you know best. Please replace my desires with the desires of your heart. Help me to make wise choices and heed the advice of those around me. Don't let me get so focused on something that I disregard your gentle guidance. Remind me that your no is not a sign that you don't love me. That no is often an answer of protection, not denial.

PAWS TO THINK

How has God telling you no turned out to be a good thing in your life?

DID YOU KNOW

Alexander the Great is said to have founded and named a city Peritas in memory of his dog.

FACING YOUR FEARS

"Do not fear, for I am with you;
do not be dismayed, for I am your God.
I will strengthen you and help you;
I will uphold you with my righteous right hand."

ISAIAH 41:10 NIV

Cosmo was a rescue animal in the truest sense of the word. My son found Cosmo as a puppy stranded on an island at a local lake. The pup had either been unable or too afraid to swim to safety and would have died if he hadn't been rescued.

Because of his past, this puppy was not a fan of any water activity. My son, on the other hand, is quite possibly part duck. He loves water activities, from swimming to kayaking to fishing. For this dog to be part of his life, he was going to have to overcome his fear.

Our son began carefully exposing Cosmo to water, taking him on walks around lakes and streams. He didn't push him, letting him get used to the fact that when his master was nearby, he was safe.

After a few weeks, they took a trip to the lake, and the puppy followed my son tentatively into the water. Turns out he was one of the few dogs who don't naturally know how to dog paddle. My very patient son helped him over that hurdle, and soon he could stay afloat on his own.

That summer, the two played in and around the water. With his dog perched on the nose of his kayak, my son paddled around the lake. They canoed, swam, and hiked. This once fearful puppy had blossomed into a confident dog who enjoyed cooling in a mountain stream on a hot day.

As I watched this process, I was struck by how closely it mirrored our own experiences with our heavenly Father. First, he rescues us from situations that lead to death. Then he gently guides us through life, and we learn that as long as he's nearby, we're never in danger. Finally, with gentle love, he helps us face our fears so we can fulfill the plans he has for us.

Dear Lord, I have so much to be thankful for. You never leave my side, no matter how timid or fearful I am. You don't ridicule me or make me feel bad. Instead, you patiently show me how pointless my fears are when you're with me. When I come up against a new fear, remind me to look back and see how far you've brought me. Let me experience victory over the things I fear. Show me again the safety that comes from walking close with you.

PAWS TO THINK

Consider things that have made you
fearful and how God helped you
find victory.

DID YOU KNOW

*All dogs can dog paddle, but not all dogs can
swim well enough to stay afloat.*

NiGHT WATCH

The eyes of the LORD are in every place,
Watching the evil and the good.

PROVERBS 15:3 NASB

Samantha came to live with us when she was a full-grown dog. She was a gorgeous mix—part golden retriever and part Irish Setter. With her sunny disposition and boundless energy, we knew she was the perfect fit for a family of boys. We intended for her to be an outside dog, but she had one unbreakable habit. That dog loved to dig. There wasn't a fence built that she couldn't tunnel under. It wasn't long before she graduated to full-time house dog. It was either that or return her to the pound. We loved her too much to let her go.

Samantha had been with us for several years when she did something odd. I was awake late one night when I heard an unusual sound coming from our front door. I softly made my way toward the front of the house.

Our front door had a glass oval set in the middle. Samantha had her nose pressed against that glass. A long growl issued from her throat as she stared into the darkness. I tiptoed to stand beside her, trying to make sure no one outside could see me. I half-expected to see someone standing on our porch, trying to break in. But no one was in sight. I tried to urge her away from the door, but she wouldn't budge, still growling and staring.

My husband joined me, and we peered into the night, trying to see what had Samantha so upset. Finally, I caught movement in the shadows at the house across the street. I pointed it out to my husband and we watched a figure removing the screen from one of the windows.

I dashed to the phone and dialed 911. The dispatcher kept me on the line until two silent police cars pulled up to our neighbor's home. By then, the intruder had slipped in the window. The police soon had the culprit well in hand.

Unbeknownst to us, our happy-go-lucky dog had kept watch every night while we slept. God does that for us too. He is always watching, protecting us from seen and unseen threats. There is sweet security in knowing that nothing can get to us unless it comes through him first. We can trust him to take care of us and those we love, and we can sleep well knowing that we have the highest security—protection for our souls.

Dear God, thank you for keeping me and my family safe. I take for granted that you are on guard every minute of every day. You never sleep, and nothing catches you unaware. I can rest, knowing that you are taking care of me. When I let fear creep in, remind me of the many times you've protected me. Let me catch a glimpse of how you have kept me from harm that I didn't know was lurking nearby. Your love knows no bounds. Keep me in perfect peace knowing you are near.

PAWS TO THINK

When was the last time you were afraid,
and God protected you?

DID YOU KNOW

*Dogs see about seven times better than humans
in low and dim light.*

CAN`T GIVE UP

We also exult in our tribulations, knowing that tribulation brings
about perseverance; and perseverance, proven character; and
proven character, hope; and hope does not disappoint, because the
love of God has been poured out within our hearts through the
Holy Spirit who was given to us.

ROMANS 5:3-5 NASB

I first met Boris the three-legged dog in Bible class. He
didn't have a lot going for him with buggy eyes, and short,
stumpy legs. He wasn't quite hairless, but he was close. In
spite of these setbacks, Boris was the happiest dog in the
neighborhood.

Boris was 100% mutt and the fastest three-legged dog
on the planet. Neither appearance nor handicap bothered
him. He loved to run, and he ran like lightning. His one
good back leg had muscles of steel and grew to twice
the size of the front two. He was ferociously territorial,
fearlessly chasing off dogs four times his size. If dogs had
mayors, Boris would have held the position in the small
town where he lived.

The school I attended held a Bible class in a small building apart from the main structure. While the teacher—who happened to be Boris' owner—expounded on Old Testament prophets, Boris put in a sudden appearance. He bounced in the door and up to the front. His tail curled the letter Q as he trotted back and forth at the professor's legs, happy to find the location where his master spent time when he was away from home. After that visit, Boris frequented our Bible class regularly, much to the chagrin of our teacher.

Paul, the author of the book of Romans, understood hardship. He faced tough work, imprisonment, beatings, stoning, shipwreck, loss at sea, danger from robbers, persecution, sleepless nights, hunger, thirst, cold, and exposure to the elements. We learn a lot about sufferings from Paul. He "exulted," or gloried, in them. Why? Because he recognized that his hard times helped him grow. They molded his character and brought hope of eternity. The rough patches taught him about the love of God. Paul gained more from struggles than he lost.

Perseverance builds character. With the help of Jesus, we can keep going, regardless of our situation. This is what Romans teaches and what a little dog in Bible class illustrated. Boris kept running. I don't think he ever realized he couldn't.

Dear Father, right now I feel like I want to give up. I'm tired and worn out. I'm not sure what you want me to do, and I'm not sure how to go on. I know that you allow hard things to come for good reasons. I know you are a good God. I know you want what is best for me. Help me to keep going and not give up. Give me perseverance to continue. Help me to endure and mold my character to be like yours. I pray for your hope and love to fill me.

PAWS TO THINK

What keeps you from giving up when you feel like it?

DID YOU KNOW

Three-legged dogs are called "tripawds."

GOOD TO BE PICKY

Each person is tempted when he is lured and enticed by his own desire. Then desire when it has conceived gives birth to sin, and sin when it is fully grown brings forth death.

JAMES 1:14-15 ESV

Lobo the German shepherd was born to protect. He'd been trained as a guard dog for the American embassy in Ecuador, where my husband's family lived. When they adopted him, he was a picky eater. His life depended on it.

Lobo ate only cooked food the family gave him. As an embassy dog, he'd been a prime target for poisoning. He was taught to refuse all other food.

Lobo's personality endeared and delighted the entire family. He understood how to play gently with five rambunctious children. He had a knack for discerning the motives and intentions of strangers. His protection gave a sense of security to everyone in the household.

But one day, Lobo got out of the yard. He explored the outside world. And then he did it again. Life beyond his gate had such a pull that his discipline began to waver. His training broke down. Tempted by other food, he quit being picky. Eventually, Lobo ate poisoned food and died.

Adam and Eve lived in a paradise of beauty and perfection in the garden of Eden. They lacked nothing, peace reigned, and death didn't exist. It all changed with the slithering temptation of Satan. Adam and Eve ate the poison of disobedience, breaking their relationship with God.

In the book of James, we discover the snake in our own garden—our wrongful desires. When fed, they birth sin, and eventually death.

Lobo knew dangers lurked outside his secure boundaries, but temptation pushed him farther and farther from safety. Lobo's problem is ours as well. When the lure of sin is nurtured, temptation is hard to resist.

I am so thankful Jesus is able to protect us from sin. He is more powerful than any temptation. He provides all that we need to say no to lures that pull us from what is right. As we spend time in his Word and learn to know him more, we develop pickiness for the right things, which helps us live obedient, fruitful lives.

Dear God, I know my tendency to wander from you. Forgive me. Help me to be picky about what I put into my mind and heart. Help me to follow your ways and desires above my own. When I am tempted, keep me from falling. Remind me to turn to you for the strength I need to resist doing things against your commands. Nurture me in your Word, that I may follow after you with my heart, mind, and soul. You are my protection each day. Thank you for being with me and wanting what is best for me.

PAWS TO THINK

Why is it that we sometimes put ourselves in the path of temptation?

DID YOU KNOW

Police dogs are trained to sniff drugs, bombs, or weapons. Their noses are about fifty times more sensitive than a human's nose.

CLOTHED

As God's chosen people, holy and dearly loved, clothe yourselves
with compassion, kindness, humility, gentleness and patience.

COLOSSIANS 3:12 NIV

Benji was an experiment. Our eight-year-old was terrified
of dogs, but we decided to give one a try. Covered in white
frizzy fur, the puppy was hard to resist. We had no idea
such a little creature would be a powerful object lesson
for all of us.

With one scoop, my husband tucked Benji under his
arm and brought him home.

"Oh, he's so cute!" a chorus of little voices exclaimed.
Six hands reached out, eager to touch him. His black
puppy eyes shone like coal jewels and his little button
nose twitched. He started squirming, and my husband put
him on the floor. His front paws waved in the air, begging
against our legs to be held.

All three of our daughters turned into little mommies
in his presence. Soon, Benji wore a doll dress and bon-
net. The girls swaddled him in blankets, pretended to

bottle-feed him, and even put a diaper on him. Too little to jump out of the doll carriage, he stood on his back legs, his front paws balanced on the rail while our daughters pushed him around town. His tiny tail wagged furiously. By all accounts, he was one happy puppy.

As cute as Benji looked dressed as a baby, Benji was still a dog. Nothing he wore and no amount of pretending could transform him into anything else.

The Apostle Paul tells us we are new creatures in Christ. Like bad clothing, our old attire included "anger, rage, malice, slander, and filthy language." Paul tells us in Colossians 3:8 that these are things to take off. They don't fit someone who follows Christ. Instead, Paul instructs us to put on a new set of clothing.

As you dress for the day, don't forget to pull on a sweater of compassion, and push your arms into kindness and humility. Button up with patience and meekness. Let forbearance and forgiveness dress you. Over all of it, put on love.

Those clothes never go out of style.

Father, because you love me, I want to live like you want me to. I get angry, and it comes out in the way I act and speak. Forgive me. Change my heart so I am compassionate, kind, and considerate to others. Clothe me with patience and humility. Fill me with your thoughts and actions, so I become more like you. Give me kindness and forgiveness for others. All these things come from you. Please take control and transform my heart to be like yours. Thank you that this is possible through Christ.

PAWS TO THINK

What can I do to encourage genuine change from bad behaviors?

DID YOU KNOW

Puppies have twenty-eight teeth and adult dogs have forty-two?

MUZZLED

We all stumble in many ways.
And if anyone does not stumble in what he says,
he is a perfect man, able also to bridle his whole body.

James 3:2 ESV

My words had poured out like molten lava, hot and fiery. Smarting at the memory of a rocky morning, I relived words I wished I could pull back. Tears blurred the approaching bus as I watched it careen around the corner. With a sigh, I moved toward it.

Orange metal doors screeched open, and I climbed the dirty steps into the Italian bus, on my way to language school. Beside me, an elderly man cradled a small dog. Across the dog's mouth, a brown muzzle acted as flexible prison bars. Above it, liquid brown eyes studied me. We sized each other up while the bus swayed, bringing us closer and then further from one another.

I need one of those, I thought, taking in the restricted jaws of the dog.

Stretched by new culture, rendered as speechless as a

child as I tried to learn this new foreign language, my frustration had spilled onto my family.

When the bus squealed into the next stop, the dog, owner, and I poured out with the rest. I moved to stand with a group of others to wait for a transfer bus. To my left, I watched the man gently lower his dog to the sidewalk.

"Let every person be quick to hear, slow to speak, slow to anger." James 1:19 ESV

James, the brother of Jesus, wrote about taming the tongue. As a leader in the Jerusalem church, James likely saw firsthand both the blessings of godly speech as well as division caused by destructive words. He challenged his readers to seek unity through disciplined conversation.

A muzzle might help, but it isn't exactly what James was suggesting.

Chastised by the image of a little dog who couldn't talk, I started planning my apology to my family. I watched the man remove his dog's muzzle. The dog stood patiently, as if he knew and accepted the required restraint for the privilege of going out with his master. Together they strolled down the sidewalk, united in the pleasure of each other's company.

Dear Father, forgive me for speaking unkind words. I am stressed, tired, and in need of your control over what I say and how I say it. Please stop my tongue before words come out that I can't take back. Open my ears to listen well. Help me not to respond rashly. I don't want anger pouring onto others. You are able to bridle my tongue, and I ask that you do. Thank you for the gift of words, and thank you for being powerful enough to tame them.

PAWS TO THINK

What helps you wait before you respond?

DID YOU KNOW

Cats weren't the only animals mummified in ancient Egypt. In catacombs south of Cairo, researchers have discovered burial sites filled with nearly eight million animals, mostly dogs.

DEVOTED TO YOU

"Because he has loved Me, therefore I will deliver him;
I will set him securely on high, because he has known My name.
He will call upon Me, and I will answer him;
I will be with him in trouble;
I will rescue him and honor him."

PSALM 91:14-15 NASB

Mom was outside hanging laundry when she heard the crunch of tires on the driveway. An old rusty Ford pickup pulled up and parked. Dad was away. Uneasiness made her glance toward the house. From where she stood, it seemed far away. The stranger's approach blocked her path to get there.

"Good afternoon. What can I do for you?" she asked.

"Is your husband home, ma'am?" Something menacing about him put her on guard. Before Mom could decide how to answer, Rin came full speed around the corner. Growling, teeth bared, and hair raised, he stood between them. The man put up his hands and backed away. "I'll come around some other time," he said.

Named after the black and white television show, Rin Tin Tin was a great judge of character.

A German shepherd, he kept farm animals in line, growled when he should, and barked when necessary. His devotion was unquestionable.

Mom never knew if the man in the Ford meant harm. She never saw him again, but Rin proved his willingness to put himself in danger's way for Mom.

Sometimes, my farmer dad had to be away for work, leaving Mom to mind the farm for a few days. Farmyards breathe and groan at night. Unintelligible sounds break the dark stillness. Animals creep and roam. She was never comfortable with the lonely nights. When dad was at home, Rin roamed the dark prairie. But every time Dad left, Rin took post under my mom's bedroom window. Mom slept well knowing Rin stood between her and harm.

Psalm 91 is a beautiful chapter, describing God as a refuge and fortress. He faithfully protects his children. We need not fear night's terrors because in the darkness, God is our guardian. He watches over us, and only what he allows touches us. Woven throughout the psalm is evidence of the Father's love. As we read God's Word and understand more of his deep care, our trust grows. We can be certain that God stands in the gap. He is worthy of our complete devotion.

Father, your love for me never fails. Thank you for answering when I call. You care about me even when I fall short of what you want for me. Sometimes, I am afraid and lonely. Everything is dark around me. You are with me when I am in trouble. Help me to remember that you are my refuge. I can run to you because you are always faithful. Thank you for all the times you protect me when I am not even aware of my need. Thank you for rescuing me.

PAWS TO THiNK

How is God showing his devoted love
for you right now?

DiD YOU KNOW

The original Rin Tin Tin, born in 1918, was a pup rescued by a serviceman on the battlefield in World War I.

SOURCES FOR DID YOU KNOW?

Page 6	care.com/c/stories/6094/101-facts-about-dogs-you-might-not-know
Page 9	dailydogdiscoveries.com/facts-about-dog-grooming
Page 12	factretriever.com/dog-facts
Page 15	thesprucepets.com/how-to-train-dog-to-wait
Page 18	beliefnet.com/entertainment/articles/interesting-facts-about-dog-shows.aspx
Page 21	scottsdalepethotel.com/why-dogs-are-so-protective-of-their-owners
Page 24	officialservicedogregistry.com/register-your-dog/therapy-dogs
Page 27	mspca.org/pet_resources/interesting-facts-about-dogs
Page 30	dogtime.com/puppies/19540-20-dog-facts-to-share-with-kids
Page 33	dogtime.com/puppies/19540-20-dog-facts-to-share-with-kids
Page 36	factretriever.com/dog-facts
Page 39	time.com/5028171/health-benefits-owning-dog
Page 42	hillspet.com/dog-care/dog-breeds/labrador-retriever
Page 45	cesarsway.com/dog-behavior/innocuous-behaviors/10-facts-about-dogs
Page 48	psychologytoday.com/us/blog/canine-corner
Page 51	foundanimals.org/why-are-dogs-loyal
Page 54	rd.com/advice/pets/dog-facts-you-didnt-know
Page 57	akc.org/dog-breeds/german-shepherd-dog
Page 60	en.wikipedia.org/wiki/Service_dog
Page 63	akc.org/expert-advice/lifestyle/10-border-collie-facts
Page 66	Chihuahuawardrobe.com/60-amazing-facts-about-Chihuahuas
Page 69	petcube.com/blog/dog-body-language/#dogtailearscommunicatingemotions
Page 72	factretriever.com/dog-facts
Page 75	akc.org/dog-breeds/shih-tzu
Page 78	cesarsway.com/dog-behavior/innocuous-behaviors/10-facts-about-dogs
Page 81	cesarsway.com/dog-behavior/innocuous-behaviors/10-facts-about-dogs
Page 84	factretriever.com/dog-facts
Page 87	dogcare.dailypuppy.com/dogs-lick-peoples-hands
Page 90	petfinder.com/dogs/bringing-a-dog-home/facts-about-new-dog
Page 93	akc.org/expert-advice/lifestyle/dog-facts
Page 96	pbs.org/independentlens/animateddogs/facts
Page 99	thevintagenews.com
Page 102	cesarsway.com/dog-behavior/innocuous-behaviors/10-facts-about-dogs
Page 105	en.wikipedia.org/wiki/Laika
Page 108	care.com/c/stories/6094/101-facts-about-dogs-you-might-not-know
Page 111	thedrakecenter.com/services/dogs/blog
Page 114	petfoodinstitute.org/pet-food-matters/nutrition-2/history-of-pet-food
Page 117	mentalfloss.com/article/68452/10-tiny-facts-about-yorkshire-terriers
Page 120	whole-dog-journal.com/issues/7_10/features
Page 123	care.com/c/stories/6094/101-facts-about-dogs-you-might-not-know
Page 126	mentalfloss.com/article/68452/10-tiny-facts-about-yorkshire-terriers
Page 129	vetstreet.com/our-pet-experts/why-does-my-dog-have-a-wet-nose
Page 132	statista.com/statistics/198100/dogs-in-the-united-states-since-2000
Page 135	akc.org/expert-advice/lifestyle/dog-facts
Page 138	factretriever.com/dog-facts
Page 141	vetstreet.com/dr-marty-becker/can-all-dogs-swim
Page 144	petmd.com/dog/slideshows/6-fascinating-facts-about-your-dogs-eyes
Page 147	tripawds.com
Page 150	easyscienceforkids.com/all-about-police-dogs
Page 153	about.com
Page 156	npr.org/2015/07/04/418079713
Page 159	npr.org/2011/09/24/140746523